ALSO BY MARVIN W. MEYER

The "Mithras Liturgy"
(editor and translator)

The Letter of Peter to Philip

Who Do People Say I Am?

The Secret Teachings of Jesus

THE SECRET TEACHINGS OF JESUS

Four Gnostic Gospels

translated,
with an introduction and notes,
by Marvin W. Meyer

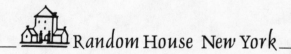Random House New York

Translation Copyright © 1984 by Marvin W. Meyer

All rights reserved under International and Pan-American
Copyright Conventions. Published in the United States by
Random House, Inc., New York, and simultaneously in Canada by
Random House of Canada Limited, Toronto.

Library of Congress Cataloging in Publication Data

Nag Hammadi codices.   English.   Selections.
   The secret teachings of Jesus.

   Includes bibliographical references.
   1. Gnosticism.   2. Jesus Christ—Teachings.   I. Meyer,
Marvin W.   II. Title.
BT1390.N33213 1984   229'.8052   84-42528
ISBN 0-394-52959-6

Manufactured in the United States of America

To Stephen and Jonathan

ⲘⲚⲦⲢⲉⲯⲖⲟ Ⲛ̄ⲂⲒ ⲠⲉⲦϢⲒⲚⲈ ⲈϤϢⲒⲚⲈ ϢⲀⲚⲦⲈϤⲂⲒⲚⲈ
ⲀⲨⲰ ϨⲞⲦⲀⲚ ⲈϤϢⲀⲚⲂⲒⲚⲈ ϤⲚⲀϢⲦⲢ̄Ⲧⲣ̄
ⲀⲨⲰ ⲈϤϢⲀⲚϢⲦⲞⲢⲦⲣ̄ ϤⲚⲀⲢ̄ ϢⲠⲎⲢⲈ
  ⲀⲨⲰ ϤⲚⲀⲢ̄ Ⲣ̄ⲢⲞ ⲈⲬⲘ̄ ⲠⲦⲎⲢϤ
                                  Gospel of Thomas saying 2

Acknowledgments

I would like to express my appreciation to several people who have assisted in the preparation of this book. The Institute for Antiquity and Christianity of Claremont Graduate School, and the Institute's director, James M. Robinson, provided a supportive context for my study of the Nag Hammadi texts translated and interpreted here. The availability of the photographic and bibliographical resources in the Institute's Nag Hammadi archive greatly aided my translational work. I have discussed portions of the translations—commonly the most difficult and perplexing passages—with students and colleagues, especially in the Claremont Coptic texts seminar, and to these friends I extend my thanks. Elaine H. Pagels, James M. Robinson, and Richard Smith have seen the entirety of the manuscript in an earlier draft, and their comments have proved particularly useful.

I also wish to acknowledge the painstaking editorial work of Beverly Haviland and Laura Schultz at Random House, and the skillful word-processing of Deborah De Golyer.

Finally, I offer my most profound expression of gratitude to my wife and children, whose loving encouragement and patience have been indispensable for the completion of this project.

Marvin W. Meyer
Ferrum College, Virginia

Contents

Introduction

In December 1945, two Egyptian *fellahin* were riding their camels, searching for natural fertilizer along the base of the magnificent cliffs that grace the Nile River as it flows around the great river bend in Upper Egypt. As one of these farmers, Muhammad Ali al-Samman Muhammad Khalifah, tells the story, they hobbled their camels and began to dig near a large boulder that lies at the foot of an exceptionally impressive cliff called the Jabal al-Tarif. Suddenly they struck something hard. They dug farther and unearthed a sealed storage jar that had lain there in the sand of Egypt for hundreds of years. At first Muhammad Ali feared to open the jar, lest he release a jinn, or spirit, imprisoned inside. Then he wondered whether the jar might not contain gold, just as other containers discovered a few kilometers upstream at the Valley of the Kings had yielded gold and treasures. His love of gold overcame his fear of jinns, and he did break open the jar. According to Muhammad Ali, indeed there was gold inside: it flew out of the jar and ascended to the sky, leaving only a collection of old papyrus books for him to throw onto his camel and take home.

The gold that Muhammad Ali saw was probably tiny papyrus fragments. Bits of papyrus, golden in color and glistening in the sun, could easily be mistaken for flecks of gold by one who hoped to find treasure. As disappointed as he might have been that day, Muhammad Ali found a real treasure, more valuable, perhaps, than a jar full of gold: a collection of ancient manuscripts, now called the Nag Hammadi library. This manuscript discovery consists of thirteen codices, or books, containing some fifty-two texts, the majority of which were previously unknown. Most of the texts reflect a mystical, esoteric religious movement that we term Gnosticism, from the Greek word *gnosis*, "knowledge." These texts are also, with a few exceptions, Christian documents, and thus they provide us with valuable new information about the character of the early church, and the Gnostic Christians within the church, during its first, formative centuries.

The Nag Hammadi manuscripts are giving us an increasingly clear perception of the Gnostic movement. Gnostics emphasized the quest for understanding, but not a common, mundane understanding; they searched for a higher knowledge, a more profound insight into the deep and secret things of God. Like other mystics, Gnostics admitted that this saving knowledge cannot be acquired through the memorization of phrases or the study of books; nevertheless, like other mystics, they composed numerous documents explaining the nature of spiritual *gnosis*. Such Gnostic texts proclaim a completely good and transcendent God, whose enlightened greatness is utterly unfathomable and essentially indescribable. Yet this divine Other can be experienced in a person's inner life, for the spirit within is actually the divine self, the inner spark or ray of heavenly light. The tragedy of human existence, however, is that most people fail to realize the fulfillment of the divine life, because of the harsh world that functions as the stage for the human drama. The Gnostics understood this mortal world, with all its evils and distractions, to be a deadly trap for one who seeks knowledge. Moreover, the divine spirit is imprisoned by the passions of the sensual soul and the elements of the fleshly body. Gnostic texts employ various figures of speech to depict the sorry fate of the entrapped spirit: it is asleep, drunk, sick, ignorant, and in darkness. In order to be liberated, then, the spirit needs to be awakened and brought to sobriety, wholeness, knowledge, and enlightenment. This transformation in one's life, Gnostics maintained, is accomplished through a call from God—the God without and within—to discover true knowledge and rest. For Gnostic Christians, the source of the divine call is Christ.

We can see why many Gnostics were considered dissidents in the ancient world. They called into question the values of "civilized" society and instead fostered spiritual values and life-styles. Some radical Gnostics apparently retreated from the world to the solitary life of the monk or the ascetic, and refused to participate in the everyday business of human society. Other equally radical Gnostics seem to have flaunted their disdain for conventional human values by disregarding the amenities of polite society and practicing a libertine way of life. Most Gnostics, however, probably led normal lives in society, while engaging in an inner, spiritual quest for God. Within the church, too, Gnostic believers often advocated a faith and life quite different from what church leaders were promoting. Gnostic Christians challenged the authority of the priests and bishops and suggested that a spiritual, Gnostic life devoted to a spiritual, Gnostic Christ allowed them to approach and embrace God directly. For their stance Gnostic Christians were eventually condemned as heretics in the debates about orthodoxy and heresy that raged within the early church, and most of their books were suppressed or destroyed by their triumphant opponents.

Consequently, before the discovery of the Nag Hammadi manuscripts, we possessed relatively few reliable sources of information on the Gnostics. Much of our information came from the hostile writings of the philosophers and theologians who tried to silence the Gnostics. Now the Nag Hammadi texts finally allow the Gnostics to speak for themselves and present their faith and theology in a fair and attractive manner.

Four of the most spectacular documents from the Nag Hammadi library are published in the present volume: the *Secret Book of James*, the *Gospel of Thomas*, the *Book of Thomas*, and the *Secret Book of John*. Of the four, two (the *Gospel of Thomas* and the *Secret Book of John*) are classics of Gnostic spirituality, known also from other manuscripts or fragments of manuscripts. All four of the works are described, in the title or the opening of the text, as secret teachings of the Savior, and reliable followers of Jesus (his brother James; Judas Thomas, regarded by some sources as Jesus' twin brother; or the spiritual disciple, John) serve as guarantors of the secret traditions. Although the precise dating of ancient documents is notoriously difficult, all four of these texts seem to have been written around the second century C.E., the *Secret Book of James* and the *Gospel of Thomas* probably being earlier than the *Book of Thomas* and the *Secret Book of John*. All four preserve older materials, and some of the recorded sayings of the Savior may go back to the historical Jesus.

The *Secret Book of James*, the *Gospel of Thomas*, and the *Book of Thomas* consist of material that was collected and edited as a part of the early church's process of working and reworking sayings of Jesus. We can see this process already in the New Testament gospels. Matthew and Luke most likely composed their gospels about fifteen to twenty years after Mark and used as their sources not only the Gospel of Mark but also a collection of Jesus' sayings. Usually referred to simply as Q (from *Quelle*, German for "source"), this collection of sayings does not exist independently as a text, but it may be reconstructed by means of a careful study of Matthew and Luke. When this is done, it becomes clear that Q was not a narrative gospel like Mark but rather a series of sayings of Jesus strung together with little or no narrative.

If Q presented Jesus as a proclaimer of wise sayings, then the *Gospel of Thomas* is a document similar to Q in form and style. Like Q, the *Gospel of Thomas* is a substantial collection of Jesus' sayings, with one saying immediately following another. In the majority of cases the only introduction to a saying is the stylized quotation formula "Jesus said." Yet, while it closely resembles Q, the *Gospel of Thomas* has been edited and revised by Christians with gnosticizing interests. It is explicitly a collection of secret sayings communicating secret wisdom, and the proper interpretation of these sayings is said to unlock the mystery of life and death (see saying 1). The *Gospel of Thomas* thus includes not only many sayings that call to mind New Testament teachings attributed to Jesus, but also others that illustrate more specifically Gnostic themes (see sayings 22, 50, 75, 113).

Already in the *Gospel of Thomas* (for example, sayings 12, 13, 22, 61, 72, 73, 77) some limited narrative framework is added to a few of the sayings, and little dialogues between Jesus and his followers are constructed. This tendency becomes more explicit in the *Secret Book of James* and the *Book of Thomas*. In these texts, sayings of Jesus are presented within more expansive discourses of Jesus (reminiscent of those in the Gospel of John), and the discourses themselves are interrupted by statements and queries of James, Peter, or Judas Thomas. The *Secret Book of James* emphasizes the place of James the Just, the brother of Jesus and hero of early Jewish Christians, and has James usurp the dominant role reserved for Peter in New Testament traditions (see such passages as 1:2; 3:1–2, 12; 5:1). The *Gospel of Thomas* claims to transcend both Jewish-Christian piety (sayings 6, 14, 27, 53, 102) and the Jewish-Christian hero James (saying 12): Judas Thomas, intoxicated with spiritual knowledge, is exalted above Peter and, by implication, James (saying 13). And it is the same Judas Thomas who also figures prominently in the *Book of Thomas*, an austere, world-renouncing text that makes use of sayings of Jesus along with motifs derived from the Greek Platonic heritage.

In these three texts Jesus' sayings are presented, interpreted, and revised within new contexts and new historical situations. Of course the interpretations and revisions show the perspectives of the second-century authors of these Christian texts, as the authors proclaim and update the Jesus tradition for a new day. At the same time, some of these sayings of Jesus must be much older than the second-century texts, and quite a few may reflect actual sayings of Jesus of Nazareth. There is no good reason to suppose that authentic sayings of Jesus are to be found only in the New Testament. They might also be found in texts like the *Secret Book of James*, the *Gospel of Thomas*, and the *Book of Thomas*.

In the present documents several sorts of sayings are especially likely to qualify as sayings of the historical Jesus. These include kingdom sayings, proverbial utterances, and parables, all of which are characteristic of the teachings of Jesus as we know them from the New Testament. For example, several parables that appear for the first time on the pages of these Nag Hammadi documents may very well come from Jesus himself: the Parable of the Palm Shoot (*Secret Book of James* 4:10–12), the Parable of the Head of Grain (*Secret Book of James* 8:2), the Parable of the Wise Fisher (*Gospel of Thomas* 8), the Parable of the Jar of Flour (*Gospel of Thomas* 95), the Parable of the Assassin (*Gospel of Thomas* 96), and at least certain features of the Parable of the Grapevine and the Weeds (*Book of Thomas* 8:2–6). Other sayings of Jesus preserved in the Nag Hammadi texts may provide us with earlier versions than the ones in the New Testament. Thus, the Parable of the Sower as presented in the *Gospel of Thomas* (saying 9) includes a storyteller's detail not found in the New Testament versions (the sower "took a handful of seeds"), but omits the later allegorical interpretation used by the church and found in each of the New Testament versions. We may infer, thanks to the discovery of the *Gospel of Thomas*, that the Parable of the Sower exists in an earlier form than that of the New Testament gospels.

The fourth and final text translated in this volume, the *Secret Book of John*, also consists of disclosures and discourses of Jesus set within the framework of a dialogue between Jesus and a disciple. The content of this text differs substantially from that of the other three documents, however, and the *Secret Book of John* contains very little, if anything, that can be considered as coming from the historical Jesus. Rather, this text is an overtly mythological account of the creation, fall, and salvation of the world and the people within the world. In its present form the account seems to be a Christianized version of an earlier Jewish text that addressed the problem of evil and vindicated the goodness of God by exegeting Genesis and other portions of the Hebrew Bible in an innovative and often shocking fashion. The obvious contrast between an absolutely excellent and all-transcendent One and an absurd and fallen world is explained through an intricate mythological account of a God who emanates, creates, falls, and finally is saved. As the plot unfolds, insights from Genesis are combined with Greek philosophical and mythological concepts to produce a richly syncretistic story. One way to read the story is as an account of the evolution of the divine Spirit, or Mind. The Spirit of all extends itself through a Thought (here in Coptic, from the Greek, *Ennoia*), a Forethought (*Pronoia*), until it achieves an enlightened spiritual Fullness (*Pleroma*). Unfortunately, a loss of Wisdom (*Sophia*) brings about a kind of Mindlessness (*Aponoia*), so that the restoration of Wisdom to wholeness of Mind can be accomplished only by means of divine Afterthought (*Epinoia*). Thus, God saves and is saved, and along with God, all of those who participate in light and spirit.

* * * *

The principal goal of this book is to provide a new English translation of these four Coptic (or late Egyptian) texts from the Nag Hammadi library. I have attempted to produce a lively translation that makes these texts accessible to the general reader. While the use of Nag Hammadi codex and page numbers should make it simpler to consult the original manuscripts, I have also divided the texts into chapters and verses. In the case of the *Gospel of Thomas* I have divided the text into sayings, but I depart from the standard numeration upon two occasions: once I combine sayings usually divided (73), and once I divide sayings usually combined (109-110). For ease of reading I have avoided using brackets to indicate textual reconstructions and restorations, but instead have sought to draw reasonable conclusions about the certainty of a translation or a restoration. In my notes I mention restorations that are particularly conjectural. The serious scholar is referred to the critical editions of the Nag Hammadi codices for a fuller discussion of the textual difficulties.

My translation is put into language that is meant to be inclusive. I have tried to be fair to the spirit of the texts while using, where possible, non-sexist terms and phrases. Thus, I use the phrase "Child of Humanity" rather than the familiar phrase "Son of Man," and "child" or "children" rather than "son" or "sons"; "person," "human (being)," or "humanity" rather than "man," unless the Coptic indicates a specifically male person; and "self" for the indefinite reflexive "himself" (so: "one who knows self" rather than "one who knows himself"). On the other hand, I have ordinarily retained the terms "father" and "mother," since such categories reflect the social world of the texts and the familial relationships among the divine characters (for example, the divine triad of Father, Mother, and Child). Since Coptic lacks the neuter gender, often employs the masculine to refer to what is indefinite or neutral, and can also use a masculine pronoun when the antecedent is a masculine epithet for a feminine character, an exact understanding of a few phrases and sections in the Coptic texts is difficult to achieve (see *Secret Book of John* 8:13 and the note describing one such instance).

Any translation is an interpretation, and so it is here. My translation builds upon the interpretive research of many of my colleagues, and I happily acknowledge my indebtedness to them. The bibliography highlights a few of the books and articles that proved helpful to me. I hope that the present translation and interpretation will help the reader study and enjoy four religious texts that are among the more exciting and significant of documents from the ancient Mediterranean world.

THE SECRET BOOK OF JAMES

Chapter 1:1 James, writing to . . .

> Peace be with you from Peace!
> Love from Love!
> Grace from Grace!
> Faith from Faith!
> Life from holy Life!

2 Since you have asked me to send you a secret book revealed to me and Peter by the Lord, I could not turn you down or refuse you. So I have written it in 3 Hebrew, and sent it to you and only you. But, considering that you are a minister for the salvation of the saints, try to be careful not to communicate this book to many people, for the Savior did not even want to communicate it to all of us, his twelve dis- 4 ciples. Nonetheless, blessed are those who will be saved through the faith of this treatise.

5 Ten months ago I sent you another secret book that the Savior revealed to me. Think of that book 6 as a revelation to me, James. As for this one, . . .

7 The twelve disciples were all sitting together, recollecting what the Savior had said to each of them, secretly or openly, and organizing their recollections into books. I, for my part, was also writing my book. 8 Behold, the Savior appeared. He had left us, and we had been watching for him.

9 Five hundred fifty days after he arose from the dead, we said to him, "Did you depart and leave us?"

10 Jesus said, "No, but I shall return to the place from which I came. If you wish to come with me, come!"

11 They all answered and said, "If you command us, we shall come."

12 He said, "I tell you the truth: no one among you will ever enter the kingdom of heaven because I commanded it, but rather because you yourselves are

13 filled. Leave James and Peter with me, that I may fill them."

14 After he summoned the two of them, he took them aside, and ordered the others to keep at their work.

Chapter 2:1 The Savior said, "You have been treated kindly. . . .

2 . . . have not understood—
do you not want to be filled?

3 Your hearts are drunk—
do you not want to be sober?
For shame!

4 "From now on, while awake or asleep, remember:
you have seen,
you have spoken with,
and you have listened to the Child of
Humanity.

5 Woe to those who have seen the Child of
Humanity!

6 Blessed are those who have not seen,
who have not associated with,
who have not spoken with,
and who have not listened to anything from
this Human Being:
life is yours!

7 "Understand this: the Child of Humanity healed you when you were sick, that you might reign.

8 Woe to those who have found rest from their
sicknesses, for they will be sick again!

9 Blessed are those who have never been sick, but
have known of rest before getting sick:
the kingdom of God is yours!

CODEX I, *pages 2–3*

MICHIGAN BULB CO.

Serving America's Gardeners Since 1943

Rosa, Royalty Hybrid Tea Rose

©1997, Michigan Bulb Company, 1950 Waldorf N.W., Grand Rapids, Michigan 49550 • Printed in the U.S.A. 35¢

Place
Stamp
Here

10   "For this reason I tell you: be filled, and let there be no empty space within you, for otherwise the one who is to come can laugh at you."

11   Then Peter answered, "Behold, three times you have told us to be filled, but we are already filled."

12   The Savior answered and said, "I have told you to be filled so that you may not lack anything, since those who are lacking will not be saved. Thus, to be

13 filled is good and to lack is bad. Yet,
> it is also good for you to be lacking,
> but bad for you to be filled.

14
> For those who are filled are also lacking,
> and one person who is lacking is not
> filled in the same way as another.
> The one who is filled, though, becomes
> sufficiently perfect.

15
> Hence, you should be lacking when you
> can be filled,
> and filled when you can be lacking,
> because then you can be filled even more.

16 So be filled with spirit but lacking in human reason,
> for human reason is only human reason,
> and the soul, too, is only soul."

Chapter 3:1   I answered and said to him, "Lord, we can obey you if you wish, for we have left our fathers, our

2 mothers, and our towns, and have followed you. But give us the means to avoid the temptation of the wicked devil."

3   The Lord answered and said, "What is your reward if you do the Father's will, but do not receive what the Father gives to those tempted by Satan?

4 But if you are afflicted and persecuted by Satan, and do the Father's will, I say this:

5
> the Father will love you,
> and make you my equal,

and think of you as having become loved ones,
through the Father's forethought,
by your free choice.

6   "Will you not forsake the love of flesh and the fear
of suffering? Do you not know?

7   You have not yet been insulted,
you have not yet been accused falsely,
you have not yet been thrown into prison,
you have not yet been condemned unjustly,
you have not yet been crucified without reason,
and you have not yet been buried in the ground,
as I was by the evil one.

8   Do you dare spare the flesh, you who have the spirit
around you like a wall?

9   Consider how long the world has
existed before you,
and how long it will last after you.
Then you will discover that your life lasts
but a single day,
and your suffering but a single hour.

10 For what is truly good will never be a part of this
world.

11   So disdain death,
but care about life.
Remember my cross and my death,
and you will live."

12   I answered and said to him, "Lord, do not speak
of your cross and death to us, for they are far from
you."

13   The Lord answered and said, "I tell you the truth:
no one will be saved who does not believe in my
cross, for the kingdom of God belongs to those who

14 believe in my cross. So seek after death as the dead
seek after life, for what the dead seek becomes
plain to them. Then what concern could they have?

CODEX I, *pages 5–6*

15 When you, likewise, inquire after death, it will teach
you about election.

16 "I tell you the truth: no one will be saved among
those who fear death. For the kingdom of death belongs to those who put themselves to death.

17   Be superior to me!
Be like the child of the holy Spirit!"

Chapter 4:1 Then I asked, "Lord, how can we prophesy to
those who ask us to prophesy to them? For many
people ask us, and expect to hear a sermon from us."

2 The Lord answered and said, "Do you not know
that the head of prophecy was removed with John?"

3 I said, "Lord, is it indeed possible to take away the
head of prophecy?"

4 The Lord said to me, "When you realize what the
head is, and that prophecy comes from the head, then
understand what this means: its head was taken
away.

5 "At first I spoke with you in parables, but you did
not understand. Now I am speaking with you plainly,

6 and you still do not perceive. Nevertheless, you served
as a parable when I spoke in parables, and as a mani-
festation when I spoke plainly.

7 "Do your best to be saved without any urging.

8 Rather, spur yourselves on, and reach the goal before
me if you can. Then the Father will love you.

9 "Hate hypocrisy and wicked thought. For such
thought produces hypocrisy, and hypocrisy is far
from truth.

10 "Do not let the kingdom of heaven waste away.
For it is like a palm shoot that dropped its dates all
around. It produced buds, and after they had grown,

11 the stalk dried up. This is what happened with the
fruit that came from this single root. After it was
harvested, more dates were produced by many new

12 shoots. It certainly would be good if this new growth
could be produced now, so that you might find the
kingdom.

13 "I was glorified like this once before. Why, then,
14 do you hold me back when I am eager to leave? After
my suffering you made me stay with you another
15 eighteen days because of the parables. For some people it was enough to listen to my teaching and to
understand these parables:
the Shepherds,
the Seed,
the Building,
the Lamps of the Young Women,
the Wages of the Workers,
the Coins,
and the Woman.

16 "Be enthusiastic about the word. For
the first aspect of the word is faith,
the second is love,
the third is good works,
and from these comes life.

17 "For the word is like a grain of wheat. After plant-
ing it, the farmer had faith in it. When it sprouted,
he loved it, for now he saw many grains instead of
18 only one. And after doing the work, he was saved:
he prepared the grain as food, and kept some out to
plant again.

19 "This is also how you can acquire the kingdom of
heaven. If you do not acquire it through knowledge,
you will not be able to find it.

Chapter 5:1 "For this reason I tell you: live soberly! Do not be
led astray! I have often told you all together, and I
2 have also told you alone, James: be saved! I have
ordered you to follow me, and I have taught you how
to act before the rulers.

3   "Take note:
        I came down,
        I spoke,
        I was afflicted,
        and I gained my crown when I saved you.

4 For I came down to dwell with you, that you also might dwell with me. But when I found your houses to be without roofs, I dwelled in other houses that could receive me when I came down.

5   "So trust in me, my friends. Understand what the
6 great light is. The Father does not need me, for a father does not need a child. Rather, a child needs
7 a father. To him I am going, for the Father of the Child does not need you.

8   "Listen to the word, understand knowledge, and love life. Then no one will persecute you and no one will oppress you, unless you do this to yourselves.

Chapter 6:1   "You miserable people! You unfortunate ones! You pretenders to truth! You falsifiers of knowledge! You
2 sinners against the spirit! Why do you continue to listen when from the beginning you should have
3 been speaking? Why do you sleep when from the beginning you should have been awake, that the
4 kingdom of heaven might receive you? I tell you the truth: it is easier for a holy person to sink into filth, and for an enlightened person to sink into darkness, than for you to reign. Is that not true?

5   "I recall your weeping, your mourning, and your
6 grief: they are far behind us. So now, you who live outside the Father's inheritance,
        weep when you should,
        and mourn,
        and preach what is good,
since the Child is ascending, as is proper.

7   "I tell you the truth: if I had been sent to people

who would listen to me, and had spoken with them,
I would never have come down to the earth. You
ought to be ashamed!

8   "Behold, I shall be leaving you. I shall go, and I
do not want to stay with you any longer, just as you
do not want this. Hurry, then, and follow me!

9   "For this reason I tell you:
I came down because of you.
You are loved ones.
You will bring life to many people.

10   Call upon the Father, pray to God frequently, and
God will give unto you.

11   Blessed is one who has seen you with God,
when God is proclaimed among the
angels and glorified among the saints:
life is yours!

12   Be happy, and rejoice as children of God. Observe
God's will, that you may be saved. Accept correction

13   from me, and save yourselves. I am mediating for
you with the Father, and the Father will forgive you
many things."

Chapter 7:1   When we heard these comments, we were delighted, for we had become gloomy because of what

2   we described earlier. But when the Lord saw that we
were happy, he said,
"Woe to you who are without a helper!
Woe to you who need grace!

3   Blessed are those who have grown confident
and have found grace for themselves!

4   "Compare yourselves with strangers. How are they
viewed in your city? Why are you anxious to banish

5   yourselves, and live far from your city? Why vacate
your dwelling, and prepare it for those who want to
live in it? You exiles and runaways!

6   Woe to you, for you will be captured!

7   "What do you think?

That the Father is a lover of humanity?
That he is influenced by prayers?
That he is gracious to one person
    because of another?
Or that he tolerates anyone who is
    seeking?

8   "For the Father knows about desire, and what the flesh needs: the flesh does not long for the soul.

9   For the body never sins apart from the soul,
        and the soul is never saved apart from the
            spirit.

10   But if the soul is saved from evil,
        and the spirit too is saved,
        then the body becomes sinless.

11   For the spirit animates the soul,
        but the body kills the soul.

In other words, the soul kills itself.

12   "I tell you the truth: the Father certainly will not forgive the sin of the soul or the guilt of the flesh.

13   For no one who has worn the flesh will be saved. Do you think that many have found the kingdom of heaven?

14   Blessed is one who envisions self as the
        fourth one in heaven!"

Chapter 8:1   When we heard these remarks, we were sad. But when the Lord saw that we were sad, he said, "For this reason I tell you this, that you may know yourselves.

2   "For the kingdom of heaven is like a head of grain growing in a field. When it was ripe, it scattered its seeds, and filled the field with heads of grain for another year.

3   "So also with you: hasten to harvest for yourselves a living head of grain, that you may be filled with the kingdom.

4   "As long as I am with you, listen to me and trust

me. But when I am far away from you, remember
5 me. Remember that I was with you and you did not
know me.

6   Blessed are those who have known me!

7   Woe to those who have heard but have not
       believed!

8   Blessed are those who have not seen but
       yet have believed!

9   "Once again I urge you: I am appearing to you
10 and building a house that is very useful to you. You
can find shelter in it, and it will remain standing
beside your neighbors' house when their house threat-
ens to collapse.

11   "I tell you the truth:
       Woe to those for whom I was sent down!

12   Blessed are those who are to ascend to the
       Father!

13   "Again I admonish you, you who exist: be like
those who do not exist, that you may dwell with those
who do not exist.

14   "Do not let the kingdom of heaven become a desert
within you. Do not be proud because of the light that
15 brings enlightenment. Rather, act toward yourselves
as I also acted toward you: I put myself under a
curse for you, that you might be saved."

Chapter 9:1   Peter responded to these comments and said,
"Lord, sometimes you urge us on toward the kingdom of heaven, but at other times you turn us away.

2 Sometimes you encourage us, draw us toward faith,
and promise us life, but at other times you throw us
out of the kingdom of heaven."

3   The Lord answered and said to us, "I have presented you with faith many times. And, James, I
revealed myself to you, but you did not know me.

4 Now again I see that often you are happy. Yet although you are delighted about the promise of life,

you are sad and gloomy when you are taught about the kingdom.

5 "Nevertheless, you have received life through faith and knowledge. So ignore words of rejection when 6 you hear them. But when you hear about the promise, rejoice all the more.

7 "I tell you the truth: whoever receives life and believes in the kingdom will never leave the kingdom, not even if the Father wishes to cast such a person out.

8 "This is all that I am going to tell you. Now I 9 shall ascend to the place from which I came. When I was eager to go, you drove me out, and instead of escorting me, you pursued me.

10 "Be attentive to the glory that is waiting for me. When you have opened your hearts, listen to the 11 hymns that await me in heaven. For today I must take my place to the right of my Father.

12 "I have spoken my last word to you. I shall be gone: a spiritual chariot has lifted me up, and now I shall strip so that I may put on clothes.

13 "Be attentive!

Blessed are those who preached the gospel
about the Child before the Child came
down:
for when I did come,
I could ascend again.

14 Blessed three times over are those who
were proclaimed by the Child before
they came into being:
for you can share salvation with them."

Chapter 10:1 When the Lord said this, he left. We (I and Peter) got on our knees and gave thanks, and sent our hearts 2 up to heaven. We heard with our ears and saw with our eyes

the noise of wars,

Codex I, pages 14–15

a trumpet blast,
and a great disturbance.

3 When we passed that place, we sent our minds
4 farther. We saw with our eyes and heard with our
ears

hymns,
angelic praises,
and angelic rejoicing.

Heavenly majesties were singing hymns, and we rejoiced, too.

5 Again after this we wished to send our spirits up
to the divine majesty. After we ascended, however,
6 we were not allowed to see or hear anything. For the
other disciples called to us and asked us, "What did
you hear from the teacher? What did he tell you?
Where did he go?"

7 We answered them, "He ascended:
he gave us his right hand,
and promised all of us life;
he showed us children coming after us,
and commanded us to love them,
since we are to be saved for their
sakes."

8 When the disciples heard this, they believed the
revelation, but they were angry about those who
9 would be born. I did not want to offend them, so I
10 sent each one of them to a different location. I myself went up to Jerusalem and prayed that I might
share salvation with the loved ones who are to appear.
11 I pray that this may begin with you. In this way I
12 can be saved, since the people of whom I speak will
be enlightened through me by my faith, and through
another faith even better than mine. For I want mine
to be the inferior faith.
13 Try, then, to be like these people, and pray that
you may share salvation with them. For the Savior

CODEX I, *pages 15–16*

gave us the revelation for the sake of the people I
14 have mentioned. On their behalf we, in turn, proclaim a share in salvation with them,

those for whom the message was proclaimed,
those whom the Lord has made his children.

THE GOSPEL OF THOMAS

or
The Secret
Sayings
of Jesus

These are the secret sayings that the living Jesus spoke and Judas Thomas the Twin recorded.

He said, "Whoever finds the interpretation of these sayings will not taste death."

Jesus said, "Let one who seeks not stop seeking until one finds.
When one finds, one will be disturbed.
When one is disturbed, one will be amazed,
and will reign over all."

Jesus said, "If your leaders say to you, 'Behold, the kingdom is in the sky,' then the birds in the sky will get there before you. If they say to you, 'It is in the sea,' then the fish will get there before you.
"Rather, the kingdom is inside you and outside you. When you know yourselves, then you will be known, and will understand that you are children of the living Father. But if you do not know yourselves, then you live in poverty, and embody poverty."

Jesus said, "The older person many days old will not hesitate to ask a little child seven days old about the realm of life, and this person will live. For many of the first will be last, and will become a single one."

Jesus said, "Know what is within your sight, and what is hidden from you will become clear to you. For there is nothing hidden that will not be revealed."

His disciples asked him and said,
"Do you want us to fast?
How shall we pray?

Shall we give to charity?
What food may we eat?"
Jesus said, "Do not lie or do what you dislike,
since all things are clear before heaven. For there is
nothing hidden that will not be revealed, and nothing covered that will not be uncovered."

Saying 7 Jesus said,
"Blessed is the lion that the human eats,
so that the lion becomes human.
Cursed is the human that the lion eats,
so that the lion becomes human."

Saying 8 He said, "A person is like a wise fisher who cast a
net into the sea, and drew it up from the sea full of
little fish. Among them the wise fisher discovered a
fine big fish. So the fisher threw all the little fish back
into the sea, and with no hesitation kept the big fish.
Whoever has ears to hear ought to listen."

Saying 9 Jesus said, "Behold, the sower went out, took a
handful of seeds, and scattered them. Some fell on
the road, and the birds came and ate them. Others
fell on rock, and they did not take root in the soil
or produce any heads of grain. Others fell among
thorns, and the thorns choked the seeds and worms
consumed them. Still others fell on good soil, and
brought forth a good crop: it yielded sixty per measure and one hundred twenty per measure."

Saying 10 Jesus said, "I have thrown fire on the world and,
behold, I am guarding it until it is ablaze."

Saying 11 Jesus said,
"This heaven will pass away,
and the heaven above it will pass away.
The dead are not alive,
and the living will not die.
During the days when you ate what is dead,
you made it alive.

CODEX II, *pages 33–34*

When you become enlightened,
what will you do?
On the day when you were one,
you became two.
But when you become two,
what will you do?"

Saying 12 The disciples said to Jesus, "We know you will leave us. Who is going to be our leader then?"

Jesus said to them, "No matter where you reside, you are to go to James the Just, for whose sake heaven and earth came into being."

Saying 13 Jesus said to his disciples, "Compare me with someone, and tell me whom I am like."

Simon Peter said to him, "You are like a just angel."

Matthew said to him, "You are like a wise philosopher."

Thomas said to him, "Teacher, my mouth is utterly unable to say whom you are like."

Jesus said, "I am not your teacher. You have become intoxicated because you have drunk from the bubbling spring that I have tended." And he took Thomas and withdrew, and told him three things.

When Thomas came back to his friends, they asked him, "What did Jesus tell you?"

Thomas said to them, "If I tell you even one of the things he told me, you will pick up rocks and stone me. Then fire will come forth from the rocks and devour you."

Saying 14 Jesus said to them,
"If you fast, you will bring sin upon
yourselves.
If you pray, you will be condemned.
If you give to charity, you will harm
your spirits.

CODEX II, *pages 34–35*

"When you go into any country and wander from place to place, and the people receive you, eat what they serve you and heal their sick. For what goes into your mouth will not contaminate you; rather, what comes out of your mouth will contaminate you."

Saying 15   Jesus said, "When you see one who was not born of a woman, bow down and worship. That is your Father."

Saying 16   Jesus said, "Perhaps people think that I have come to bring peace to the world. They do not know that I have come to bring conflict to the earth: fire, sword, war. For five people will be in a house:

it will be three against two
and two against three,
father against son
and son against father,

and they will stand alone."

Saying 17   Jesus said, "I shall give you

what no eye has seen,
what no ear has heard,
what no hand has touched,
and what has never arisen
in a human mind."

Saying 18   The disciples said to Jesus, "Tell us about the end."

Jesus said, "Have you already discovered the beginning, that now you can seek after the end? For where the beginning is, the end will be.

Blessed is one who stands at the beginning:
that one will know the end, and will not
taste death."

Saying 19   Jesus said,

"Blessed is one who came to life before
coming to life.

"If you become my disciples and hearken to my sayings, these stones will serve you.

CODEX II, *pages 35–36*

"For there are five trees in Paradise for you. They do not change, summer or winter, and their leaves do not drop. Whoever knows about them will not taste death."

Saying 20 The disciples said to Jesus, "Tell us what the kingdom of heaven is like."

He said to them, "It is like a mustard seed, the tiniest of all seeds. But when it falls on prepared soil, it grows into a large plant and shelters the birds of the sky."

Saying 21 Mary said to Jesus, "Whom are your disciples like?"

He said, "They are like little children living in a field that is not theirs. When the owners of the field come, they will say, 'Give our field back to us.' The children will take off their clothes in the presence of the owners, and thus give the field back and return it to them.

"For this reason I say: if the owner of a house knows that a thief is coming, the owner will be on guard before the thief arrives, and will not let the thief break into the house of the estate and steal the possessions.

"As for you, then, be on guard against the world. Gird yourselves and prepare for action, so that the robbers will find no way to prevail against you, for the trouble you expect will come.

"Let there be among you a person who understands. When the crop ripened, a reaper came quickly with sickle in hand and harvested it. Whoever has ears to hear ought to listen."

Saying 22 Jesus saw some babies nursing. He said to his disciples, "These nursing babies are like those who enter the kingdom."

They said to him, "Then shall we enter the kingdom as babies?"

Codex II, pages 36–37

Jesus said to them,
"When you make the two into one,
when you make the inner like the outer
and the outer like the inner,
and the upper like the lower,
when you make male and female into a
single one,
so that the male will not be male
and the female will not be female,
when you make eyes replacing an eye,
a hand replacing a hand,
a foot replacing a foot,
and an image replacing an image,
then you will enter the kingdom."

Saying 23　Jesus said, "I shall choose you,
one from a thousand
and two from ten thousand,
and these will stand as a single one."

Saying 24　His disciples said, "Show us the place where you
are, for we must seek it."
He said to them, "Whoever has ears ought to
listen. There is light within an enlightened person,
and it shines on the whole world. If the light does
not shine, it is dark."

Saying 25　Jesus said,
"Love your companion like your life,
protect such a one like the pupil of your
eye."

Saying 26　Jesus said, "You see the speck that is in your companion's eye, but you do not see the beam that is in
your own eye. When you take the beam out of your
own eye, then you will see well enough to take the
speck out of your companion's eye.

Saying 27　"If you do not fast from the world,
you will not find the kingdom.

CODEX II, *pages 37–38*

If you do not keep the Sabbath a Sabbath,
you will not see the Father."

Saying 28   Jesus said,
"I took my stand in the middle of the
world,
and in the flesh I appeared to people.
I found them all drunk,
and I did not find any of them thirsty.
My soul ached for these human children, because
they are blind of heart and do not see,
that they came into the world empty,
and they also seek to depart from the
world empty.
But now they are drunk. When they become sober,
then they will repent."

Saying 29   Jesus said, "If the flesh came into being because of
spirit, it is amazing, but if spirit came into being because of the body, it is even more amazing. I am
amazed, though, at how such great wealth has settled
into such poverty."

Saying 30   Jesus said, "Where there are three deities, they are
divine. Where there are two or one, I am present."

Saying 31   Jesus said,
"A prophet is not popular in the home town,
a doctor does not heal family and friends."

Saying 32   Jesus said, "A city founded and fortified upon a
high hill can neither fall nor be hidden."

Saying 33   Jesus said, "Preach from your roofs what you will
hear in your ear. For no one lights a lamp and then
puts it under a basket, nor does one put it in a hidden
corner. Rather, one puts it on a stand so that all
who come and go will see its light."

Saying 34   Jesus said, "If one blind person leads another blind
person, both of them will fall into a hole."

Saying 35   Jesus said, "One cannot enter the house of a strong person and take it by force without tying the owner's hands. Then one can loot the house."

Saying 36   Jesus said, "Do not worry, from morning to evening and from evening to morning, about what you will wear."

Saying 37   His disciples said, "When will you appear to us, and when shall we see you?"

Jesus said,

"When you strip
    and are not embarrassed,
  and you take your clothes
    and throw them down under your feet
      like little children
    and trample them,

then you will see the Child of the Living One and you will not be afraid."

Saying 38   Jesus said, "Often you have desired to hear these sayings that I am telling you, and you have no one else from whom to hear them. There will be days you will seek me but will not find me."

Saying 39   Jesus said, "The Pharisees and the scribes have taken the keys to knowledge and have hidden them. They have not entered, nor have they allowed those who want to enter to do so. As for you, be as clever as snakes and as innocent as doves."

Saying 40   Jesus said, "A grapevine has been planted away from the Father. Since it is not healthy, it will be pulled up by its roots and destroyed."

Saying 41   Jesus said, "Whoever has something in hand will be given more, and whoever has nothing will be deprived of even the tiny bit that person has."

Saying 42   Jesus said, "Be wanderers."

Saying 43   His disciples said to him, "Who are you to say these things to us?"

"You do not know who I am from what I say to you. Instead you have become like the Jews: either

CODEX II, *pages 39–40*

they love the tree but hate its fruit, or they love the fruit but hate the tree."

Saying 44   Jesus said, "Whoever blasphemes against the Father will be forgiven, and whoever blasphemes against the Child will be forgiven. But whoever blasphemes against the holy Spirit will not be forgiven, either on earth or in heaven."

Saying 45   Jesus said, "Grapes are not picked from thorn bushes, nor are figs gathered from thistles, for such plants yield no fruit. A good person brings forth good from the storehouse, while a bad person brings forth evil from the corrupt storehouse in the heart, and says evil things. For from the abundance of the heart this person brings forth evil."

Saying 46   Jesus said, "From Adam to John the Baptist, among those born of women, no one is so much greater than John the Baptist that one need not bow the head before John. Yet I have said that whoever among you becomes like a child will know the kingdom, and will become greater than John."

Saying 47   Jesus said, "A person cannot mount two horses or bend two bows, and a servant cannot serve two lords. That servant would respect one and offend the other.

"No person drinks aged wine and immediately wants to drink new wine. New wine is not poured into aged wineskins, for the skins may break, and aged wine is not poured into new wineskins, for the wine may spoil.

"An old patch is not sewn onto a new piece of clothing, for there would be a rip."

Saying 48   Jesus said, "If two make peace with each other in a single house, they will say to the mountain, 'Move!' and it will move."

Saying 49   Jesus said,
        "Blessed are those who are alone and chosen:
        you will find the kingdom.

For you have come from it, and you will
return there again."

Saying 50 Jesus said, "If some say to you, 'Where have you
come from?' say to them, 'We have come from the
light,

where the light came into being by itself,
established itself,
and appeared in an image of light.'

"If they say to you, 'Are you the light?' say,

'We are its children,
and we are the chosen of the living Father.'

"If they ask you, 'What is the evidence of your
Father in you?' tell them,

'It is motion and rest.' "

Saying 51 His disciples said to him, "When will the final rest
for the dead take place, and when will the new world
come?"

He said to them, "What you look for has already
come, but you do not know it."

Saying 52 His disciples said to him, "Twenty-four prophets
have spoken in Israel, and they all spoke of you."

He said to them, "You have ignored the Living
One who is with you, and have spoken only of the
dead."

Saying 53 His disciples said to him, "Is circumcision useful
or not?"

He said to them, "If it were useful, a father would
produce children already circumcised from their
mother. Rather, the true, spiritual circumcision is
useful in every respect."

Saying 54 Jesus said,

"Blessed are the poor:
yours is the kingdom of heaven."

Saying 55 Jesus said,

"Whoever does not hate father and mother
cannot be my disciple,

CODEX II, *pages 41–42*

and whoever does not hate brothers and
sisters,
and bear the cross as I do,
will not be worthy of me."

Saying 56   Jesus said,
"Whoever has come to know the world
has discovered a carcass,
and whoever has discovered a carcass
is worth more than the world."

Saying 57   Jesus said, "The kingdom of the Father is like a
person who had good seed. An enemy came at night
and sowed weeds among the good seed. The farmer
did not let the workers pull up the weeds, but said
to them, 'I fear that you will go to pull up the weeds
but will pull up the wheat along with them.' For at
harvesttime the weeds will be conspicuous, and will
be pulled up and burned."

Saying 58   Jesus said,
"Blessed is one who has suffered:
that one has found life."

Saying 59   Jesus said, "Look to the Living One as long as you
live, that you may not die and then try to see the
Living One but be unable to see."

Saying 60   They saw a Samaritan carrying a lamb and going
to Judea.
He said to his disciples, "Why is he carrying the
lamb around?"
They said to him, "So that he may kill it and eat
it."
He said to them, "He will not eat it while it is
alive, but only after it has been killed and has become
a carcass."
They said, "It cannot happen any other way."
He said to them, "So also with you: seek a place of
rest for yourselves, that you may not become a carcass
and be eaten."

CODEX II, *pages 42–43*

Saying 61   Jesus said, "Two will relax on a couch:
                       one will die,
                       one will live."
Salome said, "Who are you, sir? You sat on my couch and ate from my table as if you are somebody."
Jesus said to her,
            "I am from the One who is whole,
            I was granted my Father's estate."
Salome said, "I am your disciple."
Jesus said, "For this reason I say:
            one who is whole
                  will be filled with light,
            but one who is fragmented
                  will be filled with darkness."

Saying 62   Jesus said, "I disclose my mysteries to those who are worthy of my mysteries. Do not let your left hand know what your right hand is doing."

Saying 63   Jesus said, "There was a rich farmer who had a great deal of money. The farmer said, 'I shall invest my money so that I may sow, reap, plant, and fill my storehouses with produce. Then I shall have everything.' These were the plans, but that very night the farmer died. Whoever has ears ought to listen."

Saying 64   Jesus said, "A certain person was entertaining guests. When dinner was ready, the host sent a servant to invite the guests.

"The servant went to the first one and said, 'My lord invites you.'

"The guest said, 'Some merchants owe me money, and they are coming to me tonight. I must go to give instructions to them. Please excuse me from dinner.'

"The servant went to another guest and said, 'My lord invites you.'

"The guest said, 'I have bought a house, and I have been called away for the day. I have no time.'

"The servant went to another guest and said, 'My lord invites you.'

"The guest said, 'My friend is to be married, and I must arrange the dinner, so I shall not be able to come. Please excuse me from dinner.'

"The servant went to yet another guest and said, 'My lord invites you.'

"The guest said, 'I have bought a farm, and I am going to collect the rent, so I shall not be able to come. Please excuse me.'

"The servant returned and said to the lord, 'Those whom you invited to dinner have asked to be excused.'

"The lord said to the servant, 'Go out on the streets, and bring back whomever you find to eat my dinner.'

"Business people and merchants will not enter the realm of my Father."

Saying 65   He said, "There was a good person who owned a vineyard. The owner rented it to some farmers, that the farmers might work in it and the owner might collect the profits from them. The owner sent a servant, that the farmers might turn over the profits from the vineyard, but instead they seized, beat, and almost killed the servant. So the servant returned and told the lord. The lord said, 'Perhaps the servant did not know them.'

"The owner sent another servant, and the farmers beat that one, too.

"Then the lord sent his child and said, 'Perhaps they will show my child some respect.' But since the farmers knew that the child was the heir to the vineyard, they seized and killed the child.

"Whoever has ears ought to listen."

Saying 66   Jesus said, "Show me the stone the builders rejected: that is the cornerstone."

Saying 67   Jesus said,

CODEX II, pages 44–45

"Whoever knows everything
but lacks within
lacks everything."

Saying 68   Jesus said,
"Blessed are you when you are hated and
persecuted,
and no one will discover the place where
you have been persecuted."

Saying 69   Jesus said,
"Blessed are those who have been persecuted
in their hearts:
they truly know the Father.
"Blessed are those who are hungry,
for the stomach of the famished will be
filled."

Saying 70   Jesus said,
"If you bring forth what is within you,
what you have will save you.
If you do not have that within you,
what you do not have within you will
kill you."

Saying 71   Jesus said, "I shall destroy this house, and no one
will be able to rebuild it."

Saying 72   A person said to him, "Tell my relatives to divide
my father's property with me."

He said, "Sir, who made me a divider?"

He turned to his disciples and said to them, "I am
not a divider, am I?"

Saying 73   Jesus said, "The harvest is large but the workers
are few, so beg the Lord to send out workers to the
harvest."

Someone said, "Lord, many are around the well,
but no one is in the well."

Jesus said, "Many are standing by the door, but
those who are alone will enter the wedding chamber."

CODEX II, pages 45–46

Saying 74   Jesus said, "The kingdom of the Father is like a
merchant who had a supply of merchandise, and
then found a pearl. Now the merchant was smart:
he sold the merchandise and bought that single pearl
for himself.

> "So also with you: seek after the treasure
> > that is unfailing,
> > that is abiding,
> > where no moth comes to consume,
> > and no worm destroys."

Saying 75   Jesus said,
> "I am the light that is over all things.
> I am all:
> > all came forth from me,
> > and all attained to me.
> Split a piece of wood,
> > and I am there.
> Pick up a stone,
> > and you will find me there."

Saying 76   Jesus said, "Why have you come out to the country-
side? To see grass blown by the wind? And to see a
person dressed in rich clothing, like your rulers and
your aristocrats? They are dressed in rich clothing,
but they cannot understand truth."

Saying 77   A woman in the crowd said to him,
> > "Blessed are the womb that bore you
> > and the breasts that fed you."
> He said to her,
> > "Blessed are those who have heard the word
> > of the Father
> > and have truly kept it.
> For the time will come when you will say,
> > 'Blessed are the womb that has not conceived
> > and the breasts that have not produced
> > milk.'"

CODEX II, *pages 46–47*

Saying 78   Jesus said,
        "Whoever has come to know the world
           has discovered the body,
        and whoever has discovered the body
           is worth more than the world."

Saying 79   Jesus said,
        "Let one who is wealthy reign,
        and let one who has power renounce it."

Saying 80   Jesus said,
        "Whoever is close to me is close to the fire,
        and whoever is far from me is far from
           the kingdom."

Saying 81   Jesus said, "Images are visible to people, but the
light within is hidden in the Father's image of light.
He will reveal himself, but his image is hidden by
his light."

Saying 82   Jesus said,
        "When you see a likeness of yourself,
           you are happy.
        But when you see your images
           that came into being before you,
           and that neither die nor become visible,
        how much you will be able to tolerate!"

Saying 83   Jesus said, "Adam came from great power and
great wealth, but he was not worthy of you. For if he
had been worthy, he would not have tasted death."

Saying 84   Jesus said, "Foxes have dens and birds have nests,
but the Child of Humanity has no place to lay his
head and rest."

Saying 85   Jesus said,
        "Miserable is the body that depends on
           another body,
        and miserable is the soul that depends on
           the two of them."

Saying 86   Jesus said, "The angels and the prophets will come
to you and give you what is yours. You, in turn, give

them what you have, and say to yourselves, 'When will they come and take what is theirs?' "

Saying 87 Jesus said, "Why do you wash the outside of the cup? Do you not understand that the one who made the inside also made the outside?"

Saying 88 Jesus said, "Come to me,
for my yoke is easy
and my lordship is gentle,
and you will find rest for yourselves."

Saying 89 They said to him, "Tell us who you are so we can believe in you."

He said to them, "You study the face of the sky and the earth, but you have not come to know the one who is before you, and you do not know how to study this moment."

Saying 90 Jesus said, "Seek and you will find. In the past I did not answer all your questions. Now I am willing to answer them, but you no longer ask.

Saying 91 "Do not give what is holy to dogs,
for they may drop it on a manure pile.
Do not throw pearls to swine,
for they may make them worthless."

Saying 92 Jesus said,
"Whoever seeks will find,
whoever knocks will be let in."

Saying 93 Jesus said, "If you have money, do not lend it at interest. Rather, give it to someone who will not return it."

Saying 94 Jesus said, "The kingdom of the Father is like a woman who took a little yeast, hid it in dough, and made large loaves of bread. Whoever has ears ought to listen."

Saying 95 Jesus said, "The kingdom of the Father is like a woman who was carrying a jar full of flour. While she was walking on a road far from home, the handle of the jar broke and the flour spilled behind her on the road. She did not know it: she had not noticed the problem. When she reached her house, she put the jar down and discovered that it was empty."

Saying 96   Jesus said, "The kingdom of the Father is like someone who wanted to put a powerful person to death. He drew his sword at home and thrust it into a wall to find out whether his hand would go through. Then he killed the powerful one."

Saying 97   The disciples said to him, "Your brothers and your mother are standing outside."

He said to them, "Those here who do the will of my Father are my brothers and my mother. They will enter the kingdom of my Father."

Saying 98   They showed Jesus a gold coin and said to him, "Caesar's people demand that we pay taxes."

He said to them,

"Give Caesar what is Caesar's,
give God what is God's,
and give me what is mine.

Saying 99   "Whoever does not hate father and mother
as I do cannot be my disciple,
and whoever does not love father and
mother as I do cannot be my disciple.
For my mother . . . ,
but my true mother gave me life."

Saying 100   Jesus said, "Woe to the Pharisees, for they are like a dog sleeping in the food trough of cows: the dog neither eats nor lets the cows eat."

Saying 101   Jesus said,

"Blessed is the person who knows where
the robbers will enter.

Then the person may arise, bring the estate together, and prepare for action before the robbers break in."

Saying 102   They said to him, "Come, let us pray today, and fast."

CODEX II, *pages 49–50*

Jesus said, "What sin have I committed, or how have I failed?

"Rather, when the bridegroom leaves the wedding chamber, then let people fast and pray."

Saying 103   Jesus said, "Whoever recognizes father and mother will be called the child of a whore."

Saying 104   Jesus said,
      "When you make the two into one,
         you will become children of humanity,
      and when you say, 'Mountain, move!'
         it will move."

Saying 105   Jesus said, "The kingdom is like a shepherd who had a hundred sheep. One of them, the biggest, wandered away. The shepherd left the ninety-nine and searched for that one until it was found. After going to such trouble, the shepherd said to the sheep, 'I love you more than the ninety-nine.' "

Saying 106   Jesus said,
      "Whoever drinks from my mouth will
         be like me,
      and I shall be that person,
      and what is hidden will be revealed to
         that one."

Saying 107   Jesus said, "The kingdom is like a person who had a treasure hidden in a field but did not know it. At death the owner left the field to his child. The child did not know about the treasure either, but took over the field and sold it. The buyer went plowing and discovered the treasure, and began to lend money at interest to whomever he pleased."

Saying 108   Jesus said,
      "Let one who finds the world,
      and becomes wealthy,
         renounce the world."

Saying 109   Jesus said, "The heavens and the earth will roll up in front of you, but whoever is living on the Living One will not see death nor fear."

Saying 110   Jesus says, "Whoever finds self is worth more than the world."

Saying 111   Jesus said,
"Woe to the flesh that depends on the soul!
Woe to the soul that depends on the flesh!"

Saying 112   His disciples said to him, "When will the kingdom come?"

"It will not come by looking for it. Nor will it do to say, 'Behold, over here!' or 'Behold, over there!' Rather, the kingdom of the Father is spread out on the earth, but people do not see it."

Saying 113   Simon Peter said to them, "Let Mary leave us, because women are not worthy of life."

Jesus said, "Behold, I shall guide her so as to make her male, that she too may become a living spirit like you men. For every woman who makes herself male will enter the kingdom of heaven."

CODEX II, page 51

THE
BOOK
OF
THOMAS

or
The Secret
Sayings of
the Savior

Chapter 1:1 The secret sayings that the Savior spoke to Judas Thomas and that I, Matthew, recorded as I was walking and listening to them speak with each other.

2 The Savior said, "Brother Thomas, while you still have time in the world, listen to me and I shall explain what you have been reflecting upon in your mind.

3 "Since it is said that you are my twin and my true friend, examine yourself and understand

> who you are,
>
> how you live,
>
> and what will become of you.

4 Since you are called my brother, you should not be ignorant about yourself. I know you understand some things, for already you understand that I am

5 the knowledge of truth. While you are walking with me, though you are ignorant of other things, already you have obtained knowledge, and you will be de-

6 scribed as one who knows self. For

> whoever does not know self
>
> does not know anything,
>
> but whoever knows self
>
> already has acquired knowledge about the
>
> depth of the universe.

7 So, my brother Thomas, you have seen what is hidden from people, what they stumble over in their ignorance."

CODEX II, *page 138*

Chapter 2:1   Thomas said to the Lord, "For this reason I beg
you to tell me what I ask before your ascension.

2   When I hear from you about the things that are
hidden, then I can speak of them. For it is clear to
me that the truth is hard to accomplish in front of
people."

3   The Savior answered and said,
    "If what can be seen is obscure to you,
        how can you comprehend what cannot
            be seen?

4   If deeds of truth that are visible to the world
        are hard for you to accomplish,
            then how will you accomplish things
                that are invisible,
            things concerned with the exalted
                greatness and fullness?

5   How can you be called workers? For you are still
students, and have not yet achieved the greatness of
perfection."

6   Thomas answered and said to the Savior, "Tell us
about these things you say cannot be seen but are
hidden from us."

7   The Savior said, "All the bodies of humans and
animals are irrational from birth. Indeed, this is clear

8   from the way a creature . . . Beings that come from
above, however, do not live like the creatures you

9   can see. Rather, they derive their life from their own
root, and their crop provides nourishment for them.

10 "These bodies you can see, on the other hand,
feed on creatures like them, and for this reason they

11 are subject to change. Whatever is subject to change
will perish and be lost, and has no more hope of life,

12 because this body is an animal body. Just as animal
bodies perish, so also will these figures perish. Are
they not the result of copulation, like animal bodies?

CODEX II, *pages* 138–39

13 If this kind of body, too, is the result of copulation, how can it give birth to anything different from the animals?

14 "For this reason, then, you are babies until you attain perfection."

Chapter 3:1 Thomas answered, "That is why I tell you, Lord, that people who speak about what is invisible and hard to explain are like archers who shoot arrows at

2 a target during the night. Of course, they shoot arrows like any other archers, since they are shooting at a target, but in this case the target cannot be seen.

3 When the light comes forth, however, and banishes the darkness, then what each person has done will become clear.

4 "You are our light, and you bring enlightenment, Lord."

5 Jesus said, "Light dwells in light."

6 Thomas said, "Lord, why does this visible light that shines upon people rise and set?"

7 The Savior said, "Blessed Thomas, this visible light shines upon you not to keep you here, but to

8 make you leave. When all the chosen ones lay aside their animal nature, this light will withdraw to the realm of its being, and its being will welcome it because of its fine service."

9 Then the Savior continued and said,
   "O unsearchable love of the light!

10   O bitter fire burning within human bodies,
         in the marrow of their bones,
      burning within them night and day,
         raging within human limbs,

11   making minds drunk
         and souls deranged,
      arousing men and women day and night,
         arousing them secretly and visibly.

CODEX II, *page 139*

12 For men are aroused, and they arouse women and women arouse men.

13 "Therefore it is said, 'Everyone who seeks truth from true wisdom will fashion wings in order to fly away and escape from the passion that inflames

14 human spirits.' The seeker will fashion wings in order to escape from every spirit that can be seen."

Chapter 4:1 Thomas answered and said, "Lord, this is what I am asking, because I know you can help us, as you say."

2 The Savior answered again and said, "That is why we must speak to you, for this is instruction for those who are perfect. If you want to be perfect, you will keep these teachings. If not, you deserve to be called

3 ignorant. For a wise person cannot associate with a fool. The wise person is perfect in all wisdom, but to

4 the fool, good and evil are one and the same. For

the wise person will be nourished by truth,
and will be like a tree growing by a river.

5 "Some people have wings but run after what they
6 can see, what is far from truth. For the fire that leads them will give an illusion of truth, and will shine on

7 them with transitory beauty. It will make them prisoners of the delights of darkness, and capture them

8 in sweet-smelling pleasures. It will make them blind with unquenchable passion, it will inflame their souls, and be like a stake that is jammed into their

9 hearts and can never be removed. Or like a bit in the mouth, it directs them as it wishes.

10 "This fire has bound these people with its chains, and tied all their limbs with the bitter bond of desire for visible things, which change, and decay, and

11 fluctuate impulsively. Such people are always dragged downward. When they are put to death, they join all the filthy animals."

CODEX II, *pages 139–40*

12 Thomas answered and said, "This is clear, and has been said. . . ."

13 The Savior answered and said,
"Blessed is the wise person who seeks truth.
When one finds it, one rests upon it forever,
and is not afraid of those who want to
disturb one."

14 Thomas answered and said, "Is it good for us, Lord, to find rest among our own people?"

15 The Savior said, "Yes, it does help. It is good for you, since what is visible in human existence will
16 pass away. For the fleshly body of people will pass away, and when it disintegrates, it will find its place in what is visible and can be seen.

17 "Then the fire that those people see will make them suffer, because of their love for the faith they once had. They will be brought back to the visible
18 realm. Moreover, those people who can see in the invisible realm will be consumed, without that first love, in their concern about life and the raging of the fire.

19 "There is but a little time before what you can see will pass away. Then shapeless ghosts will come and live in the tombs among the corpses, forever bringing pain and destruction of soul."

Chapter 5:1 Thomas answered and said,
"What can we say in the face of these things?
What shall we say to people who are blind?
What instruction shall we give to these
miserable mortals?

2 They say, 'We have come to do good,
not to curse,'
but add, 'If we had not been born in
the flesh, we would not have known
about sin.' "

CODEX II, *pages 140–41*

3 The Savior said, "This is true: do not think of them as human beings, but consider them as animals.

4 For as animals devour each other, so also people like this devour each other.

5 "Moreover, the kingdom is taken from them, since
   they love the delights of fire,
   they are slaves of death,
   and they revel in filth.

6 They fulfill the lust of their parents. These people will be thrown down into hell, and will be beaten

7 as their bitter, wicked natures deserve. They will be whipped to drive them down to the unknown, and will leave the limbs of their bodies behind, not with courage but with despair.

8 "Yet these people, being foolish and mad, are

9 happy in the anxieties of this life. Some of those who rush into this madness do not realize they are foolish, but think they are wise. They are drawn to the beauty of the body, as if it would not perish.

10 Their minds turn to themselves,
   their thoughts are on their own pursuits,
   but the fire will consume them."

11 Thomas answered and said, "Lord, what will people do who are cast down in this manner? I fear for them, for many forces oppose them."

12 The Savior answered and said, "Do you not also have a visible life?"

13 Judas called Thomas said, "Lord, you should speak and I should listen."

14 The Savior answered, "Listen to what I shall say

15 to you, and believe in the truth. What sows and what is sown will pass away in fire, in fire and water, and

16 will be hidden in dark tombs. After a long time the fruit of wicked trees will appear, and will be punished and slaughtered in animal and human mouths,

CODEX II, *pages 141–42*

at the instigation of the rain, the wind, the air, and the light shining above."

Chapter 6:1 Thomas answered, "You have convinced us, Lord. We have come to this realization, and now it is clear:

2 this is as it is, and your word is sufficient for us. But these sayings that you utter are laughable and ridic-

3 ulous to the world, for they are misunderstood. How can we go forth and preach them, since the world does not respect us?"

4 The Savior answered and said, "I tell you the truth: whoever listens to what you have to say and turns away, or sneers, or smirks at these things, will be handed over to the ruler who is on high, who

5 rules as king over all the powers. The ruler will force these people to turn back, and will throw them down into hell, where they will be held in a cramped, dark

6 place. They will be unable to turn or move because of the great depth of Tartaros and the bitter burden

7 of the underworld, which holds them fast. They will be imprisoned there and will never escape, for their

8 folly will not be forgiven. The rulers who chase them will give them over to the angel Tartarouchos. Tartarouchos will take up fiery lashes, and chase them with fiery whips that spew forth sparks into the faces of those being pursued.

9 If they run toward the west, they find fire.
   If they turn south, they find it there, too.
   If they turn north, erupting fire
        threatens them again.

10 They cannot find the way to the east,
        either, to run there and be safe.

11 For while they were still embodied they did not find the way they would need to follow on the day of judgment."

Chapter 7:1 Then the Savior continued and said,

"Woe to you godless people,
who have no hope,
who hold fast to what will never happen!

2 Woe to you
who hope in the flesh,
and in the prison that will perish!

3 How long will you sleep? Or do you think that what
4 you judge to be imperishable will not perish? You
base your hope upon the world, and your god is this
life. You are destroying your souls!

5 Woe to you with the fire raging within you,
for it is unquenchable!

6 Woe to you,
because wheels are turning in your minds!

7 Woe to you,
because you are a smoldering fire inside!

8 The fire will devour your flesh visibly,
and tear your souls secretly,
and prepare you for each other!

9 Woe to you prisoners, for you are bound in
caves!

10 You laugh! You express your delight with foolish
laughter!

11 You do not realize that you will be destroyed,
you do not realize your plight,
you do not understand that you live in
darkness and death!

12 Rather, you are drunk with fire
and full of bitterness.

13 Your minds are deranged because of the
smoldering fire within you,
and you are delighted by the poisoning and
beating by your enemies!

14 Darkness has risen over you like the light,
for you have exchanged your freedom for
slavery.

CODEX II, *page 143*

15 You have made your minds dark,
you have given your thoughts over to
foolishness,
and you have choked your thoughts with the
smoke of the fire within you!

16 Your light has been hidden within a dark
cloud,
you have grown fond of the filthy clothing
you are wearing,
and you have held on to a hope that is no
hope!

17 Whom do you believe? Do you not know that you all
18 are . . . ? You baptized your souls with the water of
darkness! You rushed into whatever you desired!

19 Woe to you who live in error!

20 You do not see that the light of the sun, which judges
the universe and looks down upon the universe, will
encircle everything and make slaves of its enemies.

21 You do not realize, either, how the moon looks down
night and day and sees your slaughtered bodies.

22 Woe to you who love intercourse and filthy
association with womankind!

23 Woe to you, because the powers of your
bodies will make you suffer!

24 Woe to you on whom the evil demons act!

25 Woe to you who tempt the limbs of your
bodies with fire!

26 Who will sprinkle a cool dew upon you, to put out
27 all the burning and blazing within you? Who will
make the sun shine on you, to drive out the darkness
within you, and put the darkness and the filthy water
out of sight?

Chapter 8:1 "The sun and the moon will give a sweet smell to
you, and to
the air,
the spirit,

CODEX II, *pages* 143–44

the earth,
and the water.

2   "For if the sun does not shine on these bodies, they will waste away and die like weeds or grass. If the sun shines on weeds, they become vigorous and can
3   choke a grapevine. But if a grapevine becomes vigorous, casts its shadow over the weeds and all the rest of the brush growing along with it, and spreads and flourishes, the grapevine alone inherits the land where it grows, and dominates wherever it casts its
4   shadow. When it grows, then, it dominates the whole land, produces abundantly, and makes the
5   lord even happier. For the lord would have suffered much because of these weeds before finally pulling them out, but the grapevine disposed of them and
6   choked them all by itself. So the weeds died and became like earth."

Chapter 9:1   Then Jesus continued and said,
"Woe to you, for you have not learned
the lesson . . . , that they rise from death!

2   Blessed are you who know beforehand
about what may entrap you, and
who flee what is alien to you.

3   Blessed are you who are mocked and despised
because of the love your Lord has
for you.

4   Blessed are you who weep and are afflicted
by those without hope, for you will be
released from all that binds you.

5   "Watch and pray that you may not be born in the flesh, but that you may leave the bitter bondage of this life.

6   When you pray, you will find rest,
for you have left pain and abuse
behind.

7   When you leave bodily pains and passions,
        you will receive rest from the Good One,
        and you will reign with the King,
     you united with the King and the King
        united with you,
            now and for ever and ever.
            Amen."

THE
SECRET
BOOK
OF JOHN

Chapter 1:1   The teaching of the Savior, and the revelation of the mysteries and things hidden in silence, things that he taught to his disciple John.

2   One day, when John the brother of James (the sons of Zebedee) went up to the temple, it happened that a Pharisee named Arimanios came over to him and said to him, "Where is your teacher, whom you have been following?"

3   John said to him, "He has returned to the place from which he came."

4   The Pharisee said to him, "This Nazarene has deceived you badly, filled your ears with lies, closed your minds, and turned you away from the traditions of your parents."

5   When I, John, heard these remarks, I turned away
6   from the temple toward a place of solitude. I was very sad, and said within myself,

How was the Savior selected?
Why was he sent into the world by his
Father?
7   Who is his Father, who sent him?
To what kind of eternal realm shall we go?
8   For what was he saying when he told us,
"This eternal realm to which you will go
is a copy of the imperishable
eternal realm,"
but did not teach us what kind of
realm that one is?

9   At the moment I was thinking about this, behold,

the heavens opened, all creation under heaven lit up,
10 and the world shook. I was afraid, and behold, I saw
11 within the light a child standing by me. As I was
looking, he became like an older person. Again his
appearance changed, and was like that of a servant.
12 Not that there were several persons before me.
Rather, there was one figure with several forms
13 within the light. These different forms came into
view one after another, and three forms appeared.

14 He said to me, "John, John, why are you doubt-
ing? Why are you afraid? Are you not familiar with
this figure?

15 "Then do not be fainthearted!
I am with you always.
16 I am the Father,
I am the Mother,
I am the Child.
I am the incorruptible and the
undefiled one.
17 I have come to tell you about
what is,
what was,
and what is to come,
that you may understand what is invisible and what
is visible; and to teach you about perfect Humanity.
18 So now, lift up your head, that you may understand
the things I shall tell you today, and that you may
relate these things to your spiritual friends, who are
from the unshakable race of perfect Humanity."

Chapter 2:1 When I asked if I might understand this, he said
to me, "The One is a sovereign that has nothing over
2 it. It is God and Father of all,
the Invisible One that is over all,
that is imperishable,
that is pure light no eye can see.

Codex II, *pages 1–2*

3   "It is the invisible Spirit. One should not think of
it as a god, or like a god. For it is greater than a god,
because it has nothing over it and no lord above it.
4 It does not exist within anything that is inferior to
it, since everything exists only within it. It is eternal,
5 since it does not need anything. For it is absolutely
complete: it has never lacked anything in order to
be complete. Rather, it has always been absolutely
complete in light.

6   It is illimitable, since there is nothing
                before it to limit it.
         It is unfathomable, since there is nothing
                before it to fathom it.
7   It is immeasurable, since there was nothing
                before it to measure it.
         It is unobservable, since nothing has
                observed it.
         It is eternal, and exists eternally.
8   It is unutterable, since nothing could
                comprehend it to utter it.
         It is unnameable, since there is nothing
                before it to give it a name.

9   "It is the immeasurable light, pure, holy, bright.
It is unutterable, and is perfect in its imperishability.
10 Not that it is part of perfection, or blessedness, or
divinity: it is much greater.

11   It is neither corporeal nor incorporeal.
         It is neither large nor small.
12   It is impossible to say,
                'How much is it?'
             or 'What kind is it?'
         for no one can understand it.

13 It is not one among many things that are in exist-
14 ence: it is much greater. Not that it is actually
greater. Rather, as it is in itself, it is not a part of the

CODEX II, *pages 2–3*

worlds or of time, for whatever is part of a world was
15 once produced by something else. Time was not
allotted to it, since it receives nothing from anyone.
16 That would be a loan. The one who exists first does
not need anything from one who is later. On the
contrary, the later one looks up to the first one in its
light.
17 "For the Perfect One is majestic; it is purely and
immeasurably great.
18 It is the World that gives a world,
the Life that gives life,
the Blessed One that gives blessedness,
the Knowledge that gives knowledge,
the Good One that gives goodness,
the Mercy that gives mercy and redemption,
the Grace that gives grace.
19 Not that it is actually like this. Rather, it gives immeasurable and incomprehensible light.
20 "What shall I tell you about it? Its eternal realm
is imperishable:
it is quiet,
it is silent,
it is at rest,
and it is before everything.
21 It is the head of all the worlds, and it sustains them
through its goodness.
22 "Yet we would not know . . . , we would not understand what is immeasurable, were it not for one who
has come from the Father and has told us these
things.
Chapter 3:1 "For the Perfect One beholds itself in the light
surrounding it. This is the spring of the water of life
2 that gives forth all the worlds of every kind. The
Perfect One gazes upon its image, sees it in the spring
of the spirit, and falls in love with the luminous

water. This is the spring of pure, luminous water surrounding the Perfect One.

3   "Its Thought became active, and she who appeared in the presence of the Father in shining light came
4   forth. She is the first power: she preceded everything, and came forth from the Father's mind as the Fore-
5   thought of all. Her light resembles the Father's light; as the perfect power, she is the image of the perfect
6   and invisible virgin Spirit. She is

> the first power,
> the glory,
> Barbelo,
> the perfect glory among the worlds,
> the emerging glory.

7   She glorified and praised the virgin Spirit, for she had come forth through the Spirit.

8   "She is the first Thought, the image of the Spirit. She became the universal womb, for she precedes everything,

> the common Parent,
> the first Humanity,
> the holy Spirit,
> the triple male,
> the triple power,
> the androgynous one with three names,
> the eternal realm among the invisible beings,
> the first to come forth.

9   "Barbelo asked the invisible virgin Spirit to give her Foreknowledge, and the Spirit agreed. When the Spirit agreed, Foreknowledge appeared, and stood by Forethought. Foreknowledge comes from the
10 Thought of the invisible virgin Spirit. It glorified the Spirit and the perfect power Barbelo, for it had come into being through her.

11 "She asked again to be given Imperishability, and

CODEX II, *pages 4–5*

the Spirit agreed. When the Spirit agreed, Imperishability appeared, and stood by Thought and Fore-
12 knowledge. It glorified the Invisible One and Barbelo, for it had come into being through her.

13 "Barbelo asked to be given Life Eternal, and the
14 invisible Spirit agreed. When the Spirit agreed, Life Eternal appeared, and they stood together and glorified the invisible Spirit and Barbelo, for they had come into being through her.

15 "She asked again to be given Truth, and the in-
16 visible Spirit agreed. Truth appeared, and they stood together and glorified the good invisible Spirit and Barbelo, for they had come into being through her.

17 "This is the Father's realm of the Five. It is:
the first Humanity, the image of the
invisible Spirit, that is, Forethought,
Barbelo, Thought, along with
Foreknowledge,
Imperishability,
Life Eternal,
and Truth.

18 This is the androgynous realm of the Five, this is the realm of the Ten, this is the Father.

Chapter 4:1 "The Father entered Barbelo with a gaze, with the pure, shining light surrounding the invisible Spirit.
2 Barbelo conceived, and the Father produced a ray of light that was similar to the blessed light but not
3 as bright. This ray of light was the only Child of the common Parent that had come forth, and the only offspring and the only Child of the Father, the pure light.

4 "The invisible virgin Spirit rejoiced over the light that was produced, that came forth first from the first
5 power, Forethought, or Barbelo. The Father anointed it with goodness until it was perfectly and completely good, for the Father anointed it with the goodness

of the invisible Spirit. The Child stood in the pres-
6 ence of the Father during the anointing. When the
Child received this from the Spirit, at once it glorified the holy Spirit and the perfect Forethought, for
it had come forth through her.

7 "The Child asked to be given Mind as a companion to work with, and the invisible Spirit agreed.

8 When the Spirit agreed, Mind appeared, and stood
by Christ, and glorified Christ and Barbelo.

9 "All these beings, however, came into existence in
silence.

10 "Mind wished to create something by means
of the word of the invisible Spirit. Its Will became
a reality and appeared with Mind, while the light

11 glorified it. Word followed Will. For Christ, the
self-produced God, created everything by the word.

12 Life Eternal, Will, Mind, and Foreknowledge stood
together and glorified the invisible Spirit and Barbelo,
for they had come into being through her.

13 "The holy Spirit brought the self-produced divine

14 Child of the Spirit and Barbelo to perfection. Then
the Child could stand before the powerful and invisible virgin Spirit as the self-produced God, Christ,
whom the Spirit had honored with loud acclaim.

15 This Child came forth through Forethought. The
invisible virgin Spirit set this true, self-produced God
over everything, and caused all authority and the

16 truth within to be subject to him. Then the Child
could understand the universe that is called by a
name greater than every name, for that name will be
told only to those who are worthy of it.

Chapter 5:1   "Now

from the light, Christ,
and from Imperishability,
by the grace of the Spirit,

came the four stars that derive from the self-produced

God. He gazed about, and made the stars stand be-
2 for him. The three beings present are:

      Will,

      Thought,

      and Life.

The four powers are:

      Understanding,

      Grace,

      Perception,

      and Thoughtfulness.

3   "Grace dwells in the eternal realm of the star
Armozel, who is the first angel. These three realms
are also there:

      Grace,

      Truth,

      and Form.

4   "The second star is Oroiel, and has been appointed
over the second eternal realm. These three realms are
also there:

      Afterthought,

      Perception,

      and Memory.

5   "The third star is Daveithai, and has been appointed over the third eternal realm. These three
realms are also there:

      Understanding,

      Love,

      and Idea.

6   "The fourth eternal realm has been set up for the
fourth star, Eleleth. These three realms are also
there:

      Perfection,

      Peace,

      and Sophia.

7   "These are the four stars that stand before the self-
produced God, and the twelve eternal realms that

CODEX II, *pages 7–8*

THE SECRET BOOK OF JOHN 63

stand before the great self-produced Child, Christ,
8 by the will and grace of the invisible Spirit. The
twelve realms belong to the self-produced Child, and
thus everything was established by the will of the
holy Spirit through the self-produced one.
9 "Again,
from the Foreknowledge of the perfect Mind,
through the expressed will of the invisible
Spirit
and the will of the self-produced one,
came the perfect human, the first revelation, the
10 truth. The virgin Spirit named the human Pigeradamas, and appointed Pigeradamas to the first eternal
realm of the great self-produced one, Christ, along
11 with the first star, Armozel. The powers are there,
too. The Invisible One also gave Pigeradamas an
unconquerable power of mind.
12 "Pigeradamas glorified and praised the invisible
Spirit by saying,
'Everything has come into being through you,
and everything will return to you.
13 I shall praise and glorify you,
and the self-produced one,
and the eternal realms,
and the three,
Father,
Mother,
Child,
and perfect power.'
14 "Pigeradamas appointed a son, Seth, to the second
eternal realm, along with the second star, Oroiel.
15 "In the third eternal realm was stationed the family of Seth, with the third star, Daveithai. The souls
of the saints were stationed there.
16 "In the fourth eternal realm were stationed the
souls of those who were ignorant of the divine Full-

CODEX II, *pages 8–9*

ness. They did not repent immediately, but continued to be ignorant for a while and then repented
17 later. They are with the fourth star, Eleleth, and are creatures that glorify the invisible Spirit.

Chapter 6:1 "Now Sophia, who is the Wisdom of Afterthought and who represents an eternal realm, conceived of a thought. She had this idea herself, and the invisible
2 Spirit and Foreknowledge also reflected upon it. She wanted to give birth to a being like herself
without the permission of the Spirit (the
Spirit had not given approval),
without her lover,
and without his consideration.
3 Her partner did not give his approval; she did not find anyone who agreed with her; and she considered this matter without the Spirit's permission or any
4 knowledge of what she had decided. Nonetheless, she brought forth a child. And because of the unconquerable power within her, her thought was not
5 an idle thought. Rather, something came out of her that was imperfect and different in appearance from her, for she had produced it without her lover. It did not look like its Mother, and had a different shape.
6 "When Sophia saw what her desire had produced, it changed into the figure of a snake with the face of a lion. Its eyes were like flashing bolts of lightning.
7 She threw it away from her, outside that realm, so that none of the Immortals would see it. For she had produced it ignorantly.
8 "She surrounded it with a bright cloud, and put a throne in the middle of the cloud, so that no one would see it except the holy Spirit, who is called the
9 Mother of the Living. She named her child Yaldabaoth.

Chapter 7:1 "Yaldabaoth is the first ruler, who took great

CODEX II, *pages 9–10*

power from his Mother. Then he left her and moved
2 away from the realms where he was born. He was
strong, and created for himself other realms by means
3 of a bright flame of fire that still exists. He mated
with the Mindlessness that is in him, and produced
his own authorities:

4   The name of the first is Athoth, whom
            generations of human beings call . . .
        The second is Harmas, who is the jealous eye.
        The third is Kalila-Oumbri.
5   The fourth is Yabel.
        The fifth is Adonaios, who is called Sabaoth.
        The sixth is Cain, whom generations of
            human beings call the sun.
6   The seventh is Abel.
        The eighth is Abrisene.
        The ninth is Yobel.
7   The tenth is Armoupiael.
        The eleventh is Melcheir-Adonein.
        The twelfth is Belias, who is over the depths
            of the underworld.

8   "Yaldabaoth stationed seven kings (one for each
sphere of heaven) to reign over the seven heavens,
9 and five to reign over the depths of hell. He shared
his fire with them, but did not give away any of the
power of the light that he had taken from his Mother.
For he is a being of ignorant darkness.

10   "When the light mixed with the darkness, it made
the darkness brighter. When the darkness mixed
11 with the light, it dimmed the light. The result was
neither light nor darkness, but rather gloom.

12   "This gloomy ruler has three names:
        The first name is Yaldabaoth.
        The second is Saklas.
        The third is Samael.

13 He is wicked because of the Mindlessness that is in
him. For he said,
'I am God,
and there is no other God besides me,'
since he did not know from where his own strength
had come.

14 "The rulers created for themselves seven powers.
The powers in turn created for themselves six angels
apiece, until there were three hundred sixty-five
15 angels. These are the names of the potentates and
their corresponding physiques:

16   The first is Athoth, and has the face of
      a sheep.
    The second is Eloaios, and has the face of
      a donkey.
    The third is Astaphaios, and has the face of
      a hyena.
17   The fourth is Yao, and has the face of a
      snake with seven heads.
    The fifth is Sabaoth, and has the face of
      a dragon.
    The sixth is Adonin, and has the face of
      an ape.
18   The seventh is Sabbataios, and has a face of
      flaming fire.
This explains the seven days of the week.

19 "Yaldabaoth had many faces in addition to all of
these, so that he could show whatever face he wanted
20 when he was among the angels. He shared his fire
with them, and lorded it over them because of the
glorious power he had from his Mother's light. That
is why he called himself God, and disregarded the
realm from which he came.

21 "He united seven of his powers of thought with
the authorities that were with him. When he spoke,

CODEX II, *pages 11–12*

it was done. He named each of his powers, beginning
with the highest:

22   The first power is Goodness, and is with
            the first authority, Athoth.
        The second power is Forethought, and is
            with the second authority, Eloaios.
        The third power is Divinity, and is with
            the third authority, Astaphaios.
23   The fourth power is Lordship, and is with
            the fourth authority, Yao.
        The fifth power is Kingdom, and is with
            the fifth authority, Sabaoth.
        The sixth power is Jealousy, and is with
            the sixth authority, Adonin.
24   The seventh power is Understanding, and
            is with the seventh authority, Sabbataios.
These beings have spheres in the heavenly realms.

25   "The powers were given names from the glory
above, but these names could destroy the powers.
26 For while the names given them by their creator
were powerful, the names given them from the glory
above could bring about their destruction and loss of
power. That is why they have two names.

27   "Yaldabaoth organized everything after the pattern of the first eternal realms that had come into
being, for he wished to create beings that are like the
28 Imperishable Ones. Not that he had seen the Imperishable Ones. Rather, the power that is in him,
that he had taken from his Mother, produced the
pattern for the world order.

29   "When he saw creation all around, and the throng
of angels around him that had come forth from him,
he said to them,
            'I am a jealous God,
            and there is no other God besides me.'

30 But by making this announcement, he suggested to the angels with him that there is another God. For if there were no other God, of whom would he be jealous?

Chapter 8:1 "Then the Mother began to move around. She realized that she was lacking something when the brightness of her light diminished. She grew dim because her lover had not collaborated with her."

2 I said, "Lord, what does it mean that she moved around?"

3 The Lord laughed and said, "Do not suppose that it happened the way Moses said, 'above the waters.' No, when she recognized the wickedness that had taken place, and the robbery her son had committed,

4 she repented. Though she had become forgetful in the darkness of her ignorance, she began to be ashamed and agitated. This agitation is the moving around.

5 "The Arrogant One took power from his Mother. He was ignorant, for he thought that no other power existed except his Mother. He saw the throng of angels he had created, and exalted himself over them.

6 "When the Mother realized that this dark shadow had come into being imperfectly, she understood that her lover had not collaborated with her. She repented

7 with many tears. The whole realm of Fullness of the invisible virgin Spirit heard her prayer of repentance and offered praise for her, and the holy Spirit poured

8 some of this Fullness upon her. For her lover had not come to her before, but now he did come to her, down through the realm of Fullness, so that he might

9 restore what she lacked. She was taken up not to her own eternal realm, but instead to a position just above her son. She was to remain in this ninth heaven until she restored what was lacking in her.

10 "A voice called from the exalted heavenly realm,
'Humanity exists,
and the Child of Humanity!'

11 "The first ruler, Yaldabaoth, heard the voice and thought that it had come from his Mother. He did not realize its source.

12 It was from the holy Parent,
the completely perfect Forethought,
the image of the Invisible One,
that is, the Father of everything,
through whom everything came into being,
the first Humanity.

13 She taught these things, and revealed herself in human shape.

14 "The entire realm of the first ruler quaked, and the foundations of hell shook. The bottomside of the waters above the material world was lit up by the

15 image that had appeared. When all the authorities and the first ruler stared at this appearance, they saw the whole bottomside as it was lit up. And through the light they saw the shape of the image in the water.

Chapter 9:1 "Yaldabaoth said to the authorities with him, 'Come, let us create a human being after the image of God and with a likeness to ourselves, so that this human image may give us light.'

2 "They created with their powers, and copied the features that had appeared. Each of the authorities contributed a psychical feature corresponding to the

3 figure of the image they had seen. They created a being like the perfect first Humanity, and said, 'Let us call it Adam, that its name may give us power of light.'

4 "The powers began to create:
The first power, Goodness, created a soul of bone.

The second, Forethought, created a soul of
sinew.

The third, Divinity, created a soul of flesh.

5 The fourth, Lordship, created a soul of
marrow.

The fifth, Kingdom, created a soul of blood.

The sixth, Jealousy, created a soul of skin.

The seventh, Understanding, created a soul
of eyelid.

6 "The throng of angels stood by and received these
seven psychical substances from the authorities.
Then they could create a network of limbs and
7 trunk, with all the parts properly arranged. The first
angel began by creating the head:

Eteraphaope-Abron created the head,

Meniggesstroeth created the brain,

Asterechme the right eye,

Thaspomocha the left eye,

Yeronumos the right ear,

Bissoum the left ear,

8 Akioreim the nose,

Banen-Ephroum the lips,

Amen the teeth,

Ibikan the molars,

Basiliademe the tonsils,

Achchan the uvula,

9 Adaban the neck,

Chaaman the vertebrae,

Dearcho the throat,

Tebar the right shoulder,

. . . the left shoulder,

Mniarchon the right elbow,

. . . the left elbow,

10 Abitrion the right palm,

Euanthen the left palm,

Krus the right hand,

Beluai the left hand,
Treneu the fingers of the right hand,
Balbel the fingers of the left hand,
Krima the fingernails,
11   Astrops the right breast,
Barroph the left breast,
Baoum the right armpit,
Ararim the left armpit,
Areche the belly,
Phthaue the navel,
Senaphim the abdomen,
12   Arachethopi the right ribs,
Zabedo the left ribs,
Barias the right hip,
Phnouth the left hip,
Abenlenarchei the marrow,
Chnoumeninorin the bones,
13   Gesole the stomach,
Agromauma the heart,
Bano the lungs,
Sostrapal the liver,
Anesimalar the spleen,
Thopithro the intestines,
Biblo the kidneys,
14   Roeror the sinews,
Taphreo the back,
Ipouspoboba the veins,
Bineborin the arteries,
Atoimenpsephei the breath in all the limbs,
Enthollein all the flesh,
15   Bedouk the vagina on the right,
Arabeei the penis on the left,
Eilo the testicles,
Sorma the genitals,
Gormakaiochlabar the right thigh,
Nebrith the left thigh,

CODEX II, *page 16*

16   Pserem the muscles of the right leg,
      Asaklas the muscle on the left,
      Ormaoth the right leg,
      Emenun the left leg,
      Knux the right shin,
      Tupelon the left shin,
17   Achiel the right knee,
      Phneme the left knee,
      Phiouthrom the right foot,
      Boabel its toes,
      Trachoun the left foot,
      Phikna its toes,
      Miamai the toenails,
      Labernioum . . .
18   "The angels appointed over all these parts of the
      psychical body are:
      Athoth,
      Harmas,
      Kalila,
      Yabel,
      Sabaoth,
      Cain,
      Abel.
19   "Other angels work in the limbs:
      in the head: Diolimodraza,
      in the neck: Yammeax,
      in the right shoulder: Yakouib,
      in the left shoulder: Ouerton,
      in the right hand: Oudidi,
      in the left one: Arbao,
20   in the fingers of the right hand: Lampno,
      in the fingers of the left hand: Leekaphar,
      in the right breast: Barbar,
      in the left breast: Imae,
      in the chest: Pisandraptes,
      in the right armpit: Koade,

in the left armpit: Odeor,
21 in the right ribs: Asphixix,
in the left ribs: Sunogchouta,
in the belly: Arouph,
in the womb: Sabalo,
in the right thigh: Charcharb,
in the left thigh: Chthaon,
in all the genitals: Bathinoth,
22 in the right leg: Choux,
in the left leg: Charcha,
in the right shin: Aroer,
in the left shin: Toechea,
in the right knee: Aol,
in the left knee: Charaner,
23 in the right foot: Bastan,
in its toes: Archentechtha,
in the left foot: Marephnounth,
in its toes: Abrana.
24 "Seven angels ruled over all:
Michael,
Uriel,
Asmenedas,
Saphasatoel,
Aarmouriam,
Richram,
Amiorps.
25 "Other angels rule:
over the senses: Archendekta,
over assimilation: Deitharbathas,
over imagination: Oummaa,
over arrangement: Aachiaram,
over the whole impulse: Riaramnacho.
26 "The four sources of the demons that are in the
entire body are appointed:
heat,
cold,

wetness,

dryness,

and the mother of them all is matter.

27   The one who is lord over heat is Phloxopha,

the one who is lord over cold is Oroorrothos,

the one who is lord over what is dry is Erimacho,

the one who is lord over wetness is Athuro.

28 The mother establishes among them Onorthochras, for she is unlimited and mingles with them all. Indeed, she is matter, for through her the demons are nourished.

29   "The four principal demons are:

Ephememphi, the one of pleasure,

Yoko, the one of desire,

Nenentophni, the one of grief,

Blaomen, the one of fear.

The mother of them all is Sensation-Ouchepiptoe.

30   "From these four demons have come passions:

From grief come jealousy, envy, pain, trouble, distress, hardheartedness, anxiety, sorrow, and so forth.

31   From pleasure come much evil, vain conceit, and the like.

32   From desire come anger, wrath, bitterness, intense lust, greed, and the like.

33   From fear come terror, servility, anguish, and shame.

34 All of these passions resemble what is valuable as well as what is bad. Anaro, the head of the material soul, understands their true nature, for she dwells with Sensation-Ouchepiptoe.

35   "This is the number of angels: in all they number three hundred sixty-five. They all worked together until they completed each limb of the psychical and

36 material body. There are other angels over the remaining passions, and I have not told you about

them. If you want to know about them, the information is recorded in the Book of Zoroaster.

Chapter 10:1 "All the angels and demons worked together until they fashioned the psychical body. But for a long time their creation did not stir or move at all.

2 "When the Mother wanted to take back the power she had relinquished to the first ruler, she prayed

3 to the most merciful Parent of all. With a sacred command the Parent sent five stars down to the realm

4 of the angels of the first ruler. They advised him with this purpose in mind, that they might recover the Mother's power.

5 "They said to Yaldabaoth, 'Breathe some of your spirit into the face of Adam, and then the body will arise.'

6 "He breathed his spirit into Adam. The spirit is the power of his Mother, but he did not realize this,

7 because he lives in ignorance. Thus the Mother's power went out of Yaldabaoth, and into the psychical body that had been made to be like the One who is from the beginning.

8 "The body moved, and became powerful. And it was enlightened.

9 "At once the rest of the powers became jealous. Although Adam had come into being through all of them, and they had given their power to this human, yet Adam was more intelligent than the creators and

10 the first ruler. When they realized that Adam was enlightened, and could think more clearly than they, and was free of evil, they took and threw Adam into the lowest part of the whole material realm.

11 "The blessed, benevolent, merciful Parent had compassion for the Mother's power that had been removed from the first ruler, for the rulers might be able to overpower the psychical, sensible body once

12 again. With a benevolent spirit and great mercy the

Parent sent a helper to Adam, an enlightened After-
13 thought from the Parent, who was called Life. She
worked with all that was created,
> laboring with it,
> restoring it to fullness,
> teaching about the descent of the seed of light,
> teaching that the way of ascent is the
> same as the way of descent.

14 "Enlightened Afterthought was hidden within
Adam so that the rulers would not recognize her.
Then Afterthought would be able to restore what
the Mother lacked.

Chapter 11:1 "The human being Adam was revealed through
the bright shadow within. And Adam's ability to
2 think was greater than that of all the creators. When
they looked up, they saw that Adam's ability to think
was greater than theirs, so they devised a plan with
3 the whole throng of rulers and angels. They took
> fire,
> earth,
> and water,

and combined them with the four fiery winds. They
pounded them together, and made a great commotion.
4 "The rulers brought Adam into the shadow of
death so that they might produce a figure again, but
now from
> earth,
> water,
> fire,
> and the spirit that comes from matter,

that is, from the ignorance of darkness, and desire,
5 and their own contrary spirit. This figure is the tomb,
the newly created body that these criminals put on
6 the human as a fetter of forgetfulness. Thus Adam
became a mortal human being, the first to descend
and become estranged.

7   "The enlightened Afterthought within Adam, however, would rejuvenate Adam's mind.

8   "The rulers took Adam, and put Adam in Paradise. They said, 'Eat, and be merry!' But their pleasure is bitter and their beauty is perverse.

9   Their pleasure is a trap,
             their trees are evil,
             their fruit is deadly poison,
             their promise is death.

10   They put their Tree of Life in the middle of Paradise.

11   "I shall teach you the secret of their Life as it relates to the plan they devised and the nature of their spirit:

12   the root of their Tree is bitter,
             its branches are death,
             its shadow is hatred,
             a trap is in its leaves,
             its blossom is bad ointment,
             its fruit is death,
             desire is its seed,
             and it sprouts in darkness.

13   The dwelling place of those who taste
                of this Tree is the underworld,
             and darkness is their resting place.

14   "But the rulers stood in front of what they call the Tree of the Knowledge of Good and Evil, which is

15   actually the enlightened Afterthought. They stayed there so that Adam would not behold its fullness and thus discover Adam's own shameful nakedness.

16   "I was the one, though, who caused them to eat."

17   I said to the Savior, "Lord, was it not the snake that instructed Adam to eat?"

18   The Savior laughed and said, "The snake instructed them to eat of wickedness, pregnancy, lust, and destruction so that Adam would be of use to the

19   snake. Adam knew about the disobedience against

CODEX II, *pages 21–22*

the first ruler because the enlightened Afterthought within Adam restored Adam's mind to be greater
20 than that of the first ruler. The first ruler, in turn, wanted to recover the power that he himself had passed on to Adam. So he brought forgetfulness upon Adam."

21 I said to the Savior, "What is this forgetfulness?"

22 The Savior said, "It is not as Moses wrote and you heard. For he said in his first book, 'He caused Adam to fall asleep.' Rather, this forgetfulness made Adam
23 lose all sense. Thus the first ruler said through the prophet,

'I shall make their minds sluggish,
that they may neither understand nor discern.'

Chapter 12:1 "Then enlightened Afterthought hid herself within Adam. The first ruler wanted to take her from Adam's side, but enlightened Afterthought cannot be appre-
2 hended. While darkness pursued her, it did not apprehend her. The first ruler took out part of Adam's power, and created another figure in the form of a
3 female, like the Afterthought that had appeared. He brought forth the power that he had transferred from
4 the original human being to this female creature. It did not happen, however, the way Moses said: 'Adam's rib.'

5 "Adam saw the woman beside him. At once enlightened Afterthought appeared, and removed the
6 veil that covered his mind. The drunkenness of darkness left him. He recognized this being that was like him, and said,

'This is now bone from my bones
and flesh from my flesh!'

7 For this reason a man will leave his father and his mother, and will join himself to his wife, and the
8 two of them will become one flesh. For he will be

sent a lover, and he will leave his father and his mother.

9 "Our sister Sophia is the one who descended, in an innocent manner, to restore what she lacked. For this reason she was called Life, that is, the Mother

10 of the Living. Through sovereign Forethought and through her have the Living tasted perfect knowledge.

11 "As for me, I appeared in the form of an eagle upon the Tree of Knowledge, that is actually the Afterthought of the pure, enlightened Forethought.

12 I did this to teach the human beings, and to awaken

13 them from deep sleep. For the two of them were

14 fallen, and realized that they were naked. Afterthought, too, appeared to them as light, and awakened their minds.

Chapter 13:1 "When Yaldabaoth realized that the humans had rejected him, he cursed his earth. He found the woman as she was preparing for her husband, who

2 was lord over her. He did not know the mystery that had come into being through the sacred command.

3 The two humans were afraid to denounce Yaldabaoth, but he displayed his own ignorance to his

4 angels. He threw the humans out of Paradise, and cloaked them in thick darkness.

5 "The first ruler saw the young woman standing next to Adam, and noticed that the enlightened Afterthought of life had appeared in her. Yet Yalda-

6 baoth was full of ignorance. So when the Forethought of all realized what was happening, she dispatched emissaries, and they stole Life out of Eve.

7 "The first ruler raped Eve, and produced in her two sons, a first and a second: Elohim and Yahweh.

8 Elohim has the face of a bear,
Yahweh has the face of a cat.

CODEX II, *pages 23–24*

9   One is just,
the other is unjust.

10   He placed Yahweh over the fire and the
wind,
and he placed Elohim over the water
and the earth.

11   He called them by the names Cain and Abel, for he meant to deceive.

12   "To this day copulation has persisted because of the first ruler. He planted the lust for reproduction

13   within the woman who was with Adam. Through copulation the first ruler produced duplicate bodies, and he breathed some of his contrary spirit into them.

14   "He placed these two rulers over the elements, that they might rule over the bodily tomb.

15   "When Adam came to know what his own fore-knowledge was like, he produced a son like the Child of Humanity. He called him Seth, after the child in

16   the eternal realms. Similarly, the Mother sent down her Spirit, which is like her and is a copy of what is in the realm of Fullness, for she was about to prepare a dwelling place for the members of the eternal realms who would come down.

17   "The human beings were made to drink water of forgetfulness by the first ruler so that they would not know from where they had come. For a while

18   the seed of light was cooperative. Yet everything happened with a purpose,

that when the Spirit comes down from
the holy realms,
the Spirit may raise up the seed of light,
and heal it of what it lacks,
that the entire realm of Fullness may be
holy and lacking in nothing."

Codex II, *pages 24–25*

Chapter 14:1   I said to the Savior, "Lord, will all the souls be led safely into pure light?"

2   He answered and said to me, "These are great matters that have arisen in your mind, and it is difficult to explain them to anyone except those of the unshakable race.

3   Those upon whom the Spirit of Life will
     descend,
       and whom the Spirit will empower,
         will be saved,
         and will become perfect,
         worthy of greatness,
         and free of all evil and interest
           in wickedness,
         in that realm.

4   They are interested only in the imperishable, and they are always concerned with that,
              without anger,
              jealousy,
              envy,
              desire,
              or any greed.

5   They are affected only by their existence in the flesh, and even as they wear the flesh they look forward to the time when they will be met by those who receive

6   them. Such people are worthy of the imperishable, eternal life and calling. For they endure everything and bear everything so as to finish the contest and obtain eternal life."

7   I said to him, "Lord, what about the souls of people who have not lived in this way, but upon whom the power and the Spirit of Life have descended nonetheless? What will happen to them?"

8   He answered and said to me, "If the Spirit descends upon them, they most certainly will be saved,

CODEX II, *pages 25–26*

9 and transformed. Power must descend upon every
10 person, for without it no one could stand. After birth,
if the Spirit of Life grows, and power comes and
strengthens the soul, no one will be able to lead this
11 soul astray with evil actions. But people upon whom
the contrary spirit descends are misled by this spirit,
and lose their way."

12 I said, "Lord, where will the souls of these people
go when they leave the flesh?"

13 He laughed and said to me, "The soul that has
more power than the contemptible spirit is strong.
She escapes from evil, and through the intervention
of the Imperishable One, she is saved and is taken
up to eternal rest."

14 I said, "Lord, where will the souls go of people
who do not know to whom they belong?"

15 He said to me, "The contemptible spirit grows
stronger in such people as they lose their way. This
spirit lays a heavy burden on the soul, leads her into
evil actions, and hurls her down into forgetfulness.
16 After the soul leaves the body, she is handed over to
the authorities who have come into being through
17 the first ruler. They bind her with chains, throw
her into prison, and abuse her, until finally she
emerges from forgetfulness and acquires knowledge.
This is how she attains perfection and is saved."

18 I said, "Lord, how can the soul become youthful
again, and return into her Mother's womb, or into
Humanity?"

19 He was glad when I asked about this, and he said
to me,
"Truly blessed are you, for you understand.
20 This soul needs to follow another soul in whom the
Spirit of Life dwells, because she is saved through the
Spirit. Then she will never be thrust into flesh again."

CODEX II, *pages 26–27*

21   I said, "Lord, where will the souls go of people who once had knowledge, but then turned away?"

22   He said to me, "They will be taken to the place where the miserable angels go, where there is no repentance. They will be kept there until the day when those who have blasphemed against the Spirit will be tried, and punished eternally."

Chapter 15:1   I said, "Lord, where did the contemptible spirit come from?"

2   He said to me, "The common Parent is great in mercy,

> the universal, holy Spirit,
> the one who is compassionate
> and who labors with you—
> that is, the Afterthought of enlightened
> Forethought.

3 The Parent raised up the offspring of the perfect human generation, with the thought and the eternal
4 light of Humanity. When the first ruler realized that these people were exalted above him and could think better than he, he wanted to grasp their
5 thought. He did not know that they surpassed him in thought, so that he would be unable to grasp them.

6   "He devised a plan with his authorities, who are his powers. Together they raped Sophia, and produced something repulsive: Fate, the final, fickle bondage. Fate is like this because the powers them-
7 selves are fickle. To the present day Fate is tougher and stronger than anything else that gods, angels, demons, and all the generations of human beings
8 may confront. For from Fate have come

> all iniquity,
> injustice,
> and blasphemy,

the bondage of forgetfulness,
and ignorance,
and all burdensome orders,
weighty sins,
and great fears.

9 Thus all of creation has been blinded so that none
10 might know the God that is over them all. Because
of the bondage of forgetfulness, their sins have been
hidden. They have been bound with dimensions,
times, and seasons, and Fate is lord of all.

11 "The first ruler regretted everything that had come
into being through him. Once again he made a plan,
and decided to bring a flood upon the human world.

12 The enlightened greatness of Forethought, however,
warned Noah. He in turn announced this to the
entire human family, the children of humanity, but

13 those who were strangers did not listen to him. It
did not happen the way Moses said, 'They hid in an

14 ark.' Rather, they hid in a certain place, not only
Noah, but also many other people from the unshakable race. They entered that place and hid in a bright

15 cloud. Noah knew about his supremacy: with him
was the enlightened one who had enlightened them,
since the first ruler had brought darkness upon the
whole earth.

16 "The first ruler formulated a plan with his powers.
He sent his angels to the daughters of humanity,
that they might take women and raise a family for

17 their pleasure. At first they were unsuccessful. When
they had proven to be unsuccessful, they met again

18 and devised another plan. They created a contemptible spirit similar to the Spirit that had descended,

19 in order to adulterate souls through this spirit. The
angels then changed their appearance to look like
the partners of these women, and filled the women

with the spirit of darkness that they had concocted,
20 and with evil. They brought
> gold,
> silver,
> presents,
> copper,
> iron,
> metal,
> and all sorts of things.

21 They made the people who followed them suffer,
22 leading them astray and deceiving them. These people grew old without experiencing pleasure, and died without finding truth or knowing the God of truth.
23 In this way all of creation was forever enslaved, from the beginning of the world until now.
24 "The angels took women, and from the darkness
25 they produced children similar to their spirit. They closed their minds, and became stubborn through the stubbornness of the contemptible spirit, until the present day.

Chapter 16:1 "Now I am the perfect Forethought of all. I transformed myself into my offspring: I came into being first, and went down all the paths of life.

2 For I am the abundance of light.
I am the remembrance of fullness.

3 "I went into the realm of great darkness, and con-
4 tinued until I entered the middle of the prison. The foundations of chaos shook, and I hid from the inhabitants of chaos, for they are evil. So they did not recognize me.

5 "A second time I returned, and went on. I had come from the inhabitants of light:
I am the remembrance of Forethought.

6 I entered the middle of darkness and the center of the underworld, and turned to the task before me.

CODEX II, *pages 29–30*

7 The foundations of chaos shook, and were about to fall upon those who dwell in chaos, and destroy 8 them. I hurried back to the root of my light, that the inhabitants of chaos might not be prematurely destroyed.

9 "Yet again, a third time, I went forth:
    I am the light that dwells in light.
    I am the remembrance of Forethought.

10 I intended to enter the middle of darkness and the center of the underworld. I brightened my face with light from the consummation of this world, and entered the middle of this prison, the prison of the body.

11 "I said, 'Let whoever hears arise from deep sleep.'

12 "A sleeper wept and shed bitter tears. Wiping them away, the sleeper said, 'Who is calling my name? What is the source of this hope that has come to me, dwelling in the bondage of prison?'

13 "I said,
    'I am the Forethought of pure light.
    I am the Thought of the virgin Spirit,
        who has raised you to a place of honor.

14   Arise,
        remember that you have heard,
        and trace your root:
            for I am compassionate.

15   Guard yourself against the angels of
            misery, the demons of chaos, and
            all who entrap you,
        and beware of deep sleep, and the
            trap at the center of the underworld.'

16 "I raised the sleeper, and sealed the sleeper in luminous water with five seals, that death might not prevail from that moment on.

17 "Behold, now I shall ascend to the perfect realm.

18 I have finished discussing everything with you. I

have told you everything, for you to record and communicate secretly to your spiritual friends. For this is the mystery of the unshakable race."

19   The Savior communicated these things to John for him to record and safeguard. He said to him, "Cursed is everyone who will trade these things for a present, for food, drink, clothes, or anything else."

20   These things were communicated to John as a mystery, and afterward the Savior disappeared at

21   once. Then John went to the other disciples and reported what the Savior had told him.

Jesus Christ
Amen

NOTES

The following notes provide a brief commentary on the *Secret Book of James*, the *Gospel of Thomas*, the *Book of Thomas*, and the *Secret Book of John*. They are intended to aid the reader by explaining difficult passages, offering possible interpretations, and suggesting important parallels from ancient sources.

The Secret Book of James

Nag Hammadi Codex I, tractate 2
page 1, line 1, to page 16, line 30

Title. The text is untitled in the manuscript. The present title is supplied on the basis of 1:2 and 1:5 ("secret book," *apokryphon* in Coptic [and Greek]). Also described as a book in 1:3 and 1:7, and as a "treatise" in 1:4, the text has the framework of a letter and sometimes is provided with the title *Epistula Iacobi Apocrypha* ("Apocryphal Letter of James") in the scholarly literature.

  1:1: Salutation. "James": apparently James the Just, the brother of Jesus, although here James is made a part of the apostolic circle of the Twelve (1:3). The recipient of the letter is unknown. Since the final letters of the name survive in the manuscript (———thos), some scholars have suggested that the recipient may be none other than the famous heretic Cerinthos (see Irenaeus of Lyons, *Against Heresies* 1.26). The salutation resembles salutations and benedictions in New Testament letters, for example, Ephesians 6:23–24. For a similar series of terms (Peace, Love, Grace, Faith, Life), see the *Secret Book of John* 2:18. "Peace be with you . . .": in Hebrew, *Shalom lakem.*

  1:2–6: Occasion for the letter. 2: "Me and Peter": the order indicates rank, with James having priority over Peter (compare Galatians 2:9). "In Hebrew": most likely a literary fiction; the word "Hebrew" (*hebraiois*) still preserves, in Coptic, the Greek case-ending. 3: On the need for caution in the communication of holy books, see the

Secret Book of John 16:18–21; and especially the *Letter of Peter to James* 1.2 (in the Pseudo-Clementines): "I beg and plead with you not to communicate the books of my preachings, that I have sent you, to any of the Gentiles, nor to any of our own group before they have been tested." *5*: Nothing is known of another "Secret Book of James." *6*: Several lines of the text are damaged beyond repair.

1:7–14: Introduction to the revelatory appearance of Jesus. 7: The apostles are depicted composing their gospels and memoirs. Justin Martyr describes such "memoirs of the apostles" in *First Apology* 66.3 and *Dialogue with Trypho* 101.3; 103.8; 105.5. *9*: "Five hundred fifty days": Gnostic texts suggest various periods of time for resurrection appearances: eighteen months (that is, five hundred forty days) —the Ophites and Valentinians, according to Irenaeus; five hundred forty-five days (eighteen months plus five intercalary days?)—*Ascension of Isaiah*; or even twelve years—*Pistis Sophia, Books of Jeu*. In the New Testament, Luke-Acts is remarkably conservative in allowing only forty days, between the resurrection and the ascension, for the foundational appearances of the risen Christ. *10*: Compare John 16:5, 28, and elsewhere in John. *11*: Compare Matthew 14:28. *12*: One does not enter the kingdom by obeying commands, but rather by realizing the life of spiritual fullness. *13*: James and Peter in particular are to be filled.

2:1–16: Revelation about being filled. 1: Several lines of the text are damaged. *2–3*: Four statements showing poetic parallelism. Gnostic texts commonly describe a lack of knowledge as drunkenness, and a realization of knowledge as sobriety after drunkenness. *5–6*: Compare 8:6–8: a woe and a blessing reminiscent of John 20:29. It is later believers, who have not seen, who are truly blessed. *7*: Compare Mark 2:1–12 = Matthew 9:1–8 = Luke 5:17–26. *8–9*: Spiritual rest brings true and lasting health, and allows one to attain the kingdom. *10*: "The one who is to come" may be the person of God, or the Child of Humanity, or Christ coming with power and judgment to bring in a new world. *11*: "Three times": compare 1:12; 2:2; 2:10. *12–16*: Riddles about being filled and lacking, resolved in verse 16. One should be spiritually filled, and devoid of any preoccupation with the human intellect and the soul (*psyche*).

3:1–17: Revelation about suffering. 1: Compare Mark 10:28–30 = Matthew 19:27–29 = Luke 18:28–30. In the *Secret Book of James* the speaker is James himself; in the New Testament texts Peter speaks this line. 2: Compare Matthew 6:13 = Luke 11:4 (the Lord's Prayer). 3: Enduring temptation, James 1:12. 5: The one who endures will become like Jesus; compare John 1:12–13; 1 John 3:1–2; *Gospel of Thomas* 106. "Through the Father's forethought (*pronoia*), by your free choice": God's will and human decision go hand in hand. 7: The sufferings of Jesus (see the passion narratives in the four New Testament gospels) are the pattern for the future sufferings of believers. "Buried in the ground": literally, "in sand," as is the case in Egypt. Some scholars would emend the text to read "in shame." "By the evil one": the satanic power of this world is responsible for the sufferings of Jesus (compare 1 Corinthians 2:8; Colossians 2:15; Ephesians 6:12). 8: The spirit is a wall of fortification to protect the believers. 9: Human life and human suffering are brief, fleeting. 12: The protest of James against mention of the cross and death of Jesus may be compared with Peter's similar protest in Mark 8:32 = Matthew 16:22. 13: A theology of the cross; compare 1 Corinthians 1:18, 23, and throughout Paul. 14: Openness to death brings life. On the dead seeking life, see John 5:25. 16: "For the kingdom of death . . .": this obscure sentence seems to recommend martyrdom (unless "the kingdom of death" is taken as a critique of martyrdom as suicide). A slight emendation of the Coptic text (from *mou* to *noute*) would change the difficult phrase "kingdom of death" to "kingdom of God." 17: "Be superior to me": compare John 14:12. "The child of the holy Spirit," that is, the child of God, where the holy Spirit may be taken as God the Mother. Compare *Gospel of Thomas* 99; *Gospel of the Hebrews* fragment 3 (in Origen's *Commentary on John* 2.12.87), where Jesus refers to his Mother the Spirit.

4:1–19: Revelation about prophecy and the word. 2–4: "The head of prophecy": not only was John the Baptist beheaded (Mark 6:27–28 = Matthew 14:10–11; also Mark 6:16 = Luke 9:9), but John was considered by some early Christians as the last representative of the prophetic period (Matthew 11:12–14; Luke 16:16). 5: Compare Mark 4:33–34 = Matthew 13:34–35; John 16:25. 8: Compare 3:5, 17. 10–12: Parable of the Palm Shoot. This parable, unknown in other early Christian sources, compares the growth of a palm tree with the growth of the kingdom. From modest beginnings comes an abundant harvest; compare the Parable of the Head of Grain, 8:2. The translation of the present parable remains difficult. "Stalk" is

literally "womb," and may also be translated as "productivity." Verse
12 could be translated as follows: "It [the date palm, or the root] certainly was good: now new growth could be produced, so that you might
find it [the kingdom, most likely]." *13*: Compare John 17:5. *14*: The
interpretation of the parables, it is acknowledged, takes place after
the death of Jesus in the life of the early church. On the period of
time the risen Christ spent with the disciples, see 1:9 and the note;
the number eighteen elsewhere is associated with an eighteen-month
period of time. *15*: A collection of titles of parables. Compare the
Parables of the Shepherd and the Lost Sheep (Matthew 18:12–14 =
Luke 15:3–7 = *Gospel of Thomas* 105), the Seed (Mark 4:26–29;
Matthew 13:24–30; Mark 4:30–32 = Matthew 13:31–32 = Luke
13:18–19 = *Gospel of Thomas* 20) or the Sower (Mark 4:3–9 =
Matthew 13:3–9 = Luke 8:5–8 = *Gospel of Thomas* 9), the Houses
(Matthew 7:24–27 = Luke 6:47–49), the Wise and Foolish Young
Women (Matthew 25:1–13), the Workers in the Vineyard (Matthew
20:1–16), the Lost Coin (Luke 15:8–10), and the Woman with the
Yeast (Matthew 13:33 = Luke 13:20–21 = *Gospel of Thomas* 94)
or the Jar of Flour (*Gospel of Thomas* 95). "The Coins": probably
double drachmai. *16*: Compare the list of spiritual virtues in 1 Corinthians 13:13: faith, hope, and love. *17–18*: Parable (or Allegory) of
the Wheat and the Farmer, based on the list in verse 16.

5:1–8: Continuing revelation about salvation. 1: See 2:2–3. *2*: Compare Mark 13:9–11 = Luke 21:12–15; Matthew 10:17–20 = Luke
12:11–12. *3*: A summary of the life of Christ as a savior who descends
from heaven, gives revelation, experiences affliction, and finally is
glorified. Compare the general framework of the Gospel of John and
numerous other gnosticizing texts that proclaim a descending-
ascending savior (for instance, *Secret Book of John* 10:13; 16:1–18).
4: Compare John 1:9–13 and especially 14: the Word "tented," or
"tabernacled," among us; also John 15:4. *5*: "The great light": God
is light and Christ is light, and there is light within an enlightened
person (compare *Gospel of Thomas* 24). *8*: The enlightened believer
is free from worldly oppressions.

6:1–13: Revelation for correction and comfort. 1–3: Words of rebuke against complacency. Passive acquiescence to revelation is not
sufficient: an awareness of salvation and an active missionary program
are necessary. *4*: Compare Mark 10:25 = Matthew 19:24 = Luke
18:25. "Is that not true?": the translation is uncertain; literally, "or

not to do," which might be taken as an ironic statement ("or even not to reign!"). 5–6: Compare John 16:16–24. The ascent of the Child of God is the return to the heavenly realm, 10:1. 7: Compare John 1:10–11. 8: Discipleship involves following Christ in life and beyond. On following Christ, see the command to the disciples in Mark 1:17–18 = Matthew 4:19–20; Luke 5:10–11; also John 1:35–51. 10: Compare Mark 11:23–24 = Matthew 21:21–22; Matthew 7:7–8 = Luke 11:9–10; John 16:23–24; *Gospel of Thomas* 2; 90; 92. 11: Compare 2 Thessalonians 1:10; 1 Timothy 3:16; 1 Peter 3:18–20. 12: "Save yourselves," 1:12. 13: Compare John 14:15–17; 1 John 2:1–2.

7:1–14: *Additional revelation for correction.* 3: See 1:12; 6:12. 4–6: Believers are strangers in this world, exiles from their heavenly home. See *Gospel of Thomas* 21; *Book of Thomas* 9:2; *Secret Book of John* 5:9–14 on Pigeradamas, and throughout the text on the life of Adam and all humanity; Ephesians 2:19; Hebrews 11:13–16. 8–11: A human being is described as consisting of three parts: a body of flesh, an animal soul, and a vivifying spirit. To indulge the desires of the flesh and the animal soul is to court death, but to live on the spirit is to realize salvation for the whole person. See 2:12–16. 13: Incarnation entails wearing the flesh as a garment, and salvation is the shedding of this fleshly clothing (and sometimes the donning of a new, glorious garment). Compare 9:12; *Gospel of Thomas* 21; 37; *Book of Thomas* 7:16; *Secret Book of John* 11:1–6; Galatians 3:27; 1 Corinthians 15:42–57; 2 Corinthians 5:1–5. Few are saved, *Gospel of Thomas* 23; Matthew 22:14; Luke 13:23–24. 14: An enigmatic saying, probably meant as a blessing upon the one who understands self to be alone with God the Father, God the Mother, and God the Child.

8:1–15: *Additional revelation about saving knowledge.* 1: "Know yourself" is an ancient saying used in Greek, Christian, and Gnostic thought. Compare the inscription *Gnothi sauton,* "Know yourself," at the holy shrine of Apollo at Delphi; the discussion of this and other inscriptions in Plutarch's essay "On the E at Delphi"; Galatians 4:8–9 and 1 Corinthians 8:1–3, on knowing and being known by God; *Gospel of Thomas* 3 and *Book of Thomas* 1:5–6. Here knowing self is knowing the spirit or the divine light within. 2: Parable of the Head of Grain. The kingdom has small beginnings but yields a full harvest; compare the Parable of the Palm Shoot, 4:10–12. 6–8:

See 2:5–6; John 20:29. 9–10: Compare John 14:2–3; Matthew 7:24–
27 = Luke 6:47–49. 11: 6:7. 13: Compare 3:16: living toward death
allows one to transcend this mortal existence. 14: Compare 4:10, and
the Parable of the Palm Shoot. On the kingdom "within you," see
Gospel of Thomas 3; Luke 17:20–21. On the enlightening light, see
John 1:9. 15: Compare Galatians 3:13; Deuteronomy 21:23.

9:1–14: Conclusion of the revelation. 1–2: Reference to the alter-
nating words of encouragement and rebuke in the text. 3: The resurrection appearance to James the Just is mentioned in 1 Corinthians
15:7, and described in some detail in the Gospel of the Hebrews
fragment 7 (in Jerome's On Illustrious People 2). After the resurrection Christ appeared to James, asked for a table and bread, and
"took the bread and blessed it, and broke it and gave to James the
Just, and said to him, 'My brother, eat your bread, because the Child
of Humanity has arisen from those who sleep.'" 7: The finality of
eternal life: one who is filled with spiritual life will never be lost.
10: "The glory that is waiting for me": compare John 17:1–5; Luke
24:26; 1 Timothy 3:16; 1 Peter 1:21; 2 Peter 1:17. 11: "To the right
of my Father," that is, in a place of particular honor. The affirmation
that Christ is situated at the right hand of the Father is common in
early Christian texts, for instance, Matthew 26:64; Acts 7:55–56;
Romans 8:34. 12: The chariot was considered the usual means of
transportation to heaven. Note Elijah in 2 Kings 2:11; Enoch in
Ethiopic (1) Enoch 70:2 and Hebrew (3) Enoch 6:1; and various
figures on Roman commemorative coins. On stripping and clothing,
see 7:13 and the note. 13–14: Those who have prior knowledge of
the gospel are especially blessed. Compare also 2:9; 6:11; Gospel of
Thomas 19. According to verse 14, James and Peter share salvation
with others who are among the elect. See 10:7–14, and the later
"loved ones who are to appear," who are believers like the actual
readers to whom the text is addressed.

10:1–10: Conclusion to the revelatory appearance of Jesus. 1: The
Lord ascends to heaven, and James and Peter prepare for an ecstatic
journey. 2: Their vision is portrayed with typical apocalyptic images.
Compare the "little apocalpyse" of Mark 13:7–8 = Matthew 24:6–8
(plus verse 31) = Luke 21:9–11; also 1 Corinthians 15:52; 1 Thessalonians 4:16; Revelation 1:10 and elsewhere throughout that book,
where trumpet blasts are mentioned. 5: "The divine majesty," God:

a frequent designation among Gnostics; compare also 2 Peter 1:17; Hebrews 1:3. Here God seems to reside in the third heaven; see *Gospel of Thomas* 11. *6:* Compare *Gospel of Thomas* 13. *7:* "Children coming after us": the text is written to address readers who live some time after James and Peter but still look to Jacobean and Petrine traditions for guidance and inspiration (10:12–14). *9–10:* As leader of the Jerusalem church, James sends the disciples forth on their missionary travels to various locations. See *Gospel of Thomas* 12; Galatians 1:19; 2:1–10 along with 11–14 (people came to Antioch "from James"); Acts 12:17; 15:1–35; 21:15–26; and passages in Hegesippus (preserved in Eusebius' *History of the Church*) and the Pseudo-Clementine literature.

10:11–14: Close of the letter. *11:* The recipient of the letter ("you") is to initiate the process of enlightenment and salvation for those who will become children of the Lord. *14:* On becoming children of God, compare John 1:12–13; 1 John 3:1–2; Galatians 3:26–28; Romans 8:12–25.

The Gospel of Thomas

Nag Hammadi Codex II, tractate 2
page 32, line 10, to page 51, line 28

Title. The first of the two titles is provided in the manuscript, at the end of the text. The second, probably an earlier version of the title, is taken from the incipit, or opening of the text.

Prologue. Compare *Book of Thomas* 1:1. The "living Jesus" is Jesus as a representative and revealer of true life. Judas Thomas the Twin is literally "Didymos Judas Thomas," with the Greek (Didymos) and Syriac (Thomas) words for "twin." On Judas the brother of Jesus, see Mark 6:3 = Matthew 13:55, and on Thomas, see the four New Testament lists of the Twelve (Mark 3:16–19; Matthew 10:2–4; Luke 6:14–16; Acts 1:13), and especially John 11:16; 14:5; 20:24–29; 21:2. As elsewhere among Syriac Christians (most notably the *Book of Thomas* and the apocryphal *Acts of Thomas*), Judas is here considered to be the twin brother of Jesus, and thus the ideal figure to function as guarantor of the Jesus tradition.

1: "He said": probably Jesus, possibly Judas with an editorial note. The first saying is an invitation to search for a deeper meaning in the sayings. The interpretation (*hermeneia*, as in "hermeneutic") is the key that will unlock these frequently puzzling sayings. Compare John 8:51–52.

2: The quest for knowledge is described as a series of stages. The search will call into question comfortable suppositions about life in the world. These disturbing discoveries will lead to fresh insights, so that one finally understands oneself as exalted, crowned with knowledge and kingship. The Greek fragment Oxyrhynchus Papyrus 654 adds another stage to the series: "after reigning one will rest." These stages are also outlined in the *Book of Thomas* 4:13; 9:6–7; and the *Gospel of the Hebrews* fragment 4 (in Clement of Alexandria, *Miscellanies* [*Stromateis*] 2.9.45; 5.14.96); see also *Dialogue of the Savior* (Nag Hammadi Codex III, tractate 5), page 129, lines 14–16; Matthew 7:7–8 = Luke 11:9–10.

3: Compare 51; 89; 112. A satirical critique of announcements that the kingdom of God is coming as an external, political, worldly entity. Rather, the kingdom comes with the knowledge of self and of God. On knowing self, see the *Secret Book of James* 8:1 and the note. The kingdom "in the sea" (the Greek fragment Oxyrhynchus Papyrus 654 has "under the earth") refers to the subterranean waters of the abyss. See Deuteronomy 30:11–14; Romans 10:6–8; Luke 17:20–21.

4: A Jewish boy was usually circumcised on the eighth day; compare Genesis 17:12. Here a child, so innocent that he has not yet been circumcised, communicates knowledge; compare Matthew 11:25–26 = Luke 10:21. On the reversal, compare Mark 10:31 = Matthew 19:30; 20:16; Luke 13:30. "Single one": an integrated existence that transcends all the divisive categories of human life (compare 11; 22; 23; 104).

5: Compare Mark 4:22 = Luke 8:17; Matthew 10:26 = Luke 12:2. The Greek fragment Oxyrhynchus Papyrus 654 adds "and nothing buried that will not be raised." A similar reference to burial and resurrection is also found on a Christian shroud of the fifth or sixth century; compare 1 Corinthians 15:20–22.

6: The disciples raise questions about Jewish or Jewish-Christian observance of the law; compare 14; 27; 53; 102; Matthew 6:1–18. Here Jesus ignores external commands and emphasizes that one is to live in accordance with the promptings of the heart. "Do not . . . do what you dislike" is a paraphrase of the golden rule. Compare Rabbi

Hillel in the Babylonian Talmud, *Shabbath* 31a; Tobit 4:15; Matthew 7:12 = Luke 6:31; also the command to love one's neighbor as oneself, Mark 12:31 = Matthew 22:39 = Luke 10:27 (citing Leviticus 19:18); Matthew 19:19; Romans 13:8; James 2:8. "For there is nothing hidden . . .": see 5.

7: On the lion, compare Yaldabaoth in the *Secret Book of John* 6:6. On eating and being eaten, see 11; 60. If the lion (a symbol for the world of flesh and death) eats a human, this is an accursed matter, because then humanity is assimilated to the lion. On the other hand, if a human being eats the lion, this is a blessed occurrence, because then the bestial becomes human. For other statements of the transformation inherent in salvation, see 22 (becoming one); 106 (becoming Christ); 113 (becoming male).

8: Parable of the Wise Fisher. Compare the Parable of the Fishing Net, Matthew 13:47–50. "A person": literally "the human" (in other words, "the wise person"); as uttered by the historical Jesus this parable would probably begin "The kingdom is like . . ." "Whoever has ears . . . ," that is, "listen carefully": an invitation to the reader to find the real interpretation of the saying. Compare 21; 24; 63; 65; 94; Mark 4:9, 23; Matthew 11:15; 13:9, 43; Luke 8:8; 14:35; Revelation 2:7; 13:9.

9: Parable of the Sower, Mark 4:3–9 = Matthew 13:3–9 = Luke 8:5–8. Only the parable is presented here, without the allegorical amplifications of the New Testament versions.

10: Compare Luke 12:49: Jesus as judge.

11: A series of four riddles. On the two heavens passing away, compare Mark 13:31 = Matthew 24:35 = Luke 21:33; Matthew 5:18; Luke 16:17; 1 Corinthians 7:31; 1 John 2:17; and 2 Corinthians 12:2–4, on the third heaven, "Paradise," as the realm of God. On eating and vivifying the dead, compare 7 and the note. On becoming one and becoming two, compare especially 22; also 4 and the note.

12: A Jewish-Christian statement affirming the central role and exalted position of James the Just, the brother of Jesus. Compare *Secret Book of James* 10:9–10 and the note for those verses. The honorary description of James as one "for whose sake heaven and earth came into being" is a Jewish expression used to praise holy people.

13: Compare the events on the road to Caesarea Philippi, Mark 8:27–33 = Matthew 16:13–23 = Luke 9:18–22. Here Judas the

Twin exceeds Peter and Matthew in insight, and the juxtaposition of saying 13 and saying 12 suggests that here the role of Judas is understood as also transcending that of his brother James. "I am not your teacher" (or "master"): Jesus serves the drink, but it is the believer who must partake and become intoxicated with knowledge. Compare 106; Secret Book of James 4:7–8; Secret Book of John 16:11–16. The "three things" told to Judas Thomas are unknown but presumably must be matters that ordinary believers would consider blasphemous, and hence punishable by stoning.

14: Another saying opposing Jewish or Jewish-Christian forms of piety (fasting, praying, giving alms). Compare 6; 27; 53; 102. For the second part of the saying about the life of the wandering disciple (compare 42), see Luke 10:8–9 = Matthew 10:8; 1 Corinthians 10:27; plus Mark 7:15 = Matthew 15:11.

15: The phrase "born of a woman" designates human birth; compare Galatians 4:4.

16: Compare Luke 12:49–53 = Matthew 10:34–36. The word for "alone" is the Greek term *monachos*, used to describe one who is single, independent, at one with self (compare 49; 73). The term may also denote "monk." See 4 and the note, on the related term "single one."

17: Compare the wisdom saying in 1 Corinthians 2:9 (see Isaiah 64:4).

18: To return to the beginning is to discover the end. Compare 49; Secret Book of John 5:12.

19: True life comes not from physical birth but from the prior spiritual life (see 99; also John 1:1–5, 14). On stones that serve a useful function, see Matthew 3:9 = Luke 3:8; Matthew 4:3 = Luke 4:3; Luke 19:40, and Habakkuk 2:11. The five living trees of Paradise are known from other Gnostic texts, for example, Pistis Sophia; compare also Genesis 2:9; Revelation 2:7; 22:2; Secret Book of John 11:8–15.

20: Parable of the Mustard Seed, Mark 4:30–32 = Matthew 13: 31–32 = Luke 13:18–19.

21: A description of the life of discipleship. The first part of this saying maintains that the true disciple gives up bodily and worldly attachments. The removal of clothing seems to be linked, in a symbolic way, to the release of one's claim upon a piece of property. On the second part of the saying, see Matthew 24:43 = Luke 12:39; Mark 3:27 = Matthew 12:29 = Luke 11:21–22. On the third part, see Luke 12:35–37. "Gird yourselves and prepare for action": literally, "Gird your loins with great strength." Girding the loins involved the hitching up of clothing in preparation for activity. On the fourth part of the saying, see Joel 3:13; Mark 4:29. "Whoever has ears . . .": see 8 and the note.

22: Another saying that begins by likening believers to young children; compare Mark 9:33–37 = Matthew 18:1–5 = Luke 9:46–48; Mark 10:13–16 = Matthew 19:13–15 = Luke 18:15–17. On the naive question of the disciples, compare Nicodemus as "straight man" in John 3:4. Salvation is the transformation of one's fragmented life into a unified wholeness; see the *Gospel of the Egyptians* fragment 5 (in Clement of Alexandria, *Miscellanies [Stromateis]* 3.13.92), which employs motifs reflected also in *Gospel of Thomas* saying 37 (trampling on clothing); 2 *Clement* 12:2; *Acts of Peter* 38. In the New Testament, compare the baptismal formula in Galatians 3:27–28; also 1 Corinthians 12:13; Colossians 3:11; Ephesians 2:14–16.

23: Compare Matthew 22:14; Ecclesiastes 7:28; *Secret Book of James* 7:13–14.

24: "Whoever has ears . . .": see 8 and the note. "It shines," or "the person shines." The eyes are the windows of the mind, and light shines into and out of a person through the eyes. Compare Matthew 6:22–23 = Luke 11:34–36.

25: "Companion": literally "brother." "Life": literally "soul," probably a Semitism. Compare the command to love one's neighbor, Leviticus 19:18 (see above, the note to saying 6); and Deuteronomy 32:10; Psalm 17:8; Proverbs 7:2; Sirach 17:22.

26: Compare Matthew 7:3–5 = Luke 6:41–42.

27: A saying that interprets true fasting and true Sabbath-observance as abstinence and rest from the world. Keeping "the Sabbath a [true] Sabbath" may also be understood as keeping "the [whole] week a Sabbath." For other reevaluations of Jewish or Jewish-Christian piety, see 6; 14; 53; 102.

28: Compare the *Secret Book of James* 2:2–3. In Gnostic texts one who is ignorant and unaware is often described as drunk.

29: This saying marvels at the close relationship between the spirit, on the one hand, and flesh and body, on the other. The spirit ("such great wealth") exists in the flesh ("such poverty"), and may also lead the body to salvation. See 7 and the note; also 83; 85; 111; *Secret Book of James* 7:8–11.

30: Compare Matthew 18:20. The saying as preserved in Oxyrhynchus Papyrus 1 may possibly be restored to read as follows: "Where there are three, they are without God. Where there is a single one, I say, I am present." On the person who is alone, at one with God, see 4 and 16, with the notes.

31: Compare Mark 6:4 = Matthew 13:57 = Luke 4:23–24; John 4:44.

32: Compare Matthew 5:14; 7:24–25 = Luke 6:47–48.

33: The Coptic adds, after "in your ear," the phrase "in the other ear." This addition probably is an instance of dittography, but could be taken to have an esoteric meaning, namely that one must be open to a special Gnostic "hearing" of the text. Compare Matthew 10:27 = Luke 12:3; Mark 4:21 = Luke 8:16; Matthew 5:15 = Luke 11:33.

34: Compare Matthew 15:14 = Luke 6:39.

35: Compare 21; Mark 3:27 = Matthew 12:29 = Luke 11:21–22.

36: Compare Matthew 6:25 = Luke 12:22.

37: The vision of discipleship. See 21 and 22, with the notes; also Genesis 2:25 and 3:7, on nakedness and the absence or presence of shame. The clause "When you strip and are not embarrassed [or ashamed]" may also be translated "When you strip yourselves of your shame."

38: Compare Matthew 13:17 = Luke 10:24; 17:22; Mark 2:20 = Matthew 9:15 = Luke 5:35; John 7:33–36; saying 59.

39: Compare Matthew 23:13 = Luke 11:52; Matthew 10:16 (on snakes and doves). On the same general theme, see saying 100.

40: A judgment saying like Matthew 15:13; John 15:6; the Parable of the Grapevine and the Weeds (*Book of Thomas* 8:2–6); or the Parable of the Wheat and the Weeds (saying 57; Matthew 13:24–30).

41: Compare Mark 4:24–25 = Matthew 13:12 = Luke 8:18; Matthew 25:29 = Luke 19:26.

42: Other possible translations of this brief and fascinating saying are the following: "Come into being as you pass away" (compare 2 Corinthians 4:16; *Secret Book of James* 3:13–16); and "Become passersby" (that is, live as strangers in the world). The translation "Be wanderers" may be compared with descriptions of wandering charismatic missionaries in Mark 6:7–13 = Matthew 10:5–15 = Luke 9:1–6; 10:1–12; *Didache* 11–13.

43: Compare Matthew 7:16–20 = Luke 6:43–44; Matthew 12:33.

44: Compare Mark 3:28–29 = Matthew 12:31–32 = Luke 12:10.

45: See Luke 6:44–45, where references to fruit harvested and merchandise stored are brought together in a similar way; also Matthew 7:16–20; 12:34–35.

46: Compare Matthew 11:11 = Luke 7:28. "Bow the head before John": literally, "break (or lower) the eyes," in deference or respect.

47: On the first part, see Matthew 6:24 = Luke 16:13; on the second, Mark 2:22 = Matthew 9:17 = Luke 5:37–39; on the third, Mark 2:21 = Matthew 9:16 = Luke 5:36.

48: Compare 104; Matthew 18:19; Mark 11:23 = Matthew 21:21; Matthew 17:20 = Luke 17:6; 1 Corinthians 13:2.

49: Compare 18; 50; *Secret Book of John* 5:12.

50: One of the most overtly mythological sayings in the entire text, saying 50 parallels much of what is discussed in detail in the *Secret Book of John*. Believers ultimately derive their existence from the light above. The divine light came into existence independently, and eventually showed itself in "an image of light" (literally, "their image"). Believers are the children of this divine light, and they themselves are enlightened with an inner light ("your Father in you," compare 24) that enables them both to move (compare *Secret Book of John* 10:8) and to rest from life's labors.

51: A denial of the new world as something reserved only for the future: the new world has already come. The present reality of the new realm of life is a common theme in various Gnostic and gnosticizing texts: the last judgment occurs in the present (John 3:18–19), and the resurrection, too, is already here (compare John 5:25; 1 Corinthians 15:12; 2 Timothy 2:17–18; *Treatise on Resurrection* [Nag Hammadi Codex I, tractate 4]). In general, see also Luke 17:20–21; in the present text, sayings 3 and 112.

52: A preoccupation with prophecy and fulfillment distracts one from the real object of attention, "the Living One who is with you." Compare John 5:39–40. The twenty-four prophets may be the twenty-four books of the Hebrew canon, the "Old" Testament, according to one means of counting (2 Esdras 14:45).

53: A critique of the efficacy of circumcision. Compare 6; 14; 27; 102. On spiritual circumcision, see Romans 2:25–29.

54: Compare especially Luke 6:20, also Matthew 5:3 (for the phrase "kingdom of heaven").

55: Compare 99; Mark 8:34–35 = Matthew 16:24–25 = Luke 9:23–24; Matthew 10:37–38 = Luke 14:26–27.

56: To discover that the world is only a dead body is to liberate oneself from the world. Also see 78.

57: Parable of the Wheat and the Weeds: compare Matthew 13: 24–30.

58: Compare Matthew 5:10–12 = Luke 6:22–23; James 1:12; 1 Peter 3:14; *Secret Book of James* 3:1–17.

59: Compare John 13:33; *Secret Book of James* 8:4–8; saying 38.

60: A saying on consuming and being consumed: compare 7.

61: On the first portion, see Luke 17:34; also Matthew 24:40–41 = Luke 17:34–35. "As if you are somebody": the Coptic literally reads "as if from one." In the ancient Mediterranean world guests ordinarily reclined on couches for formal meals. The comments on wholeness and fragmentation emphasize the need to be an integrated, unified person, just as God is truly One. ("Salome said" and "Jesus said" are added for clarity.) See the "single one" in 4; 11; 22; 23; 104; as well as the discussion about being filled and lacking, in the *Secret Book of James* 2:12–16. In the *Secret Book of John*, as elsewhere in Gnostic literature, the fullness of the divine light is contrasted with the diminution and deficiency of the light fallen into this world (5:16; 7:10–11; 8:1, 6–9; 13:18).

62: The first sentence is partially restored; compare Mark 4:11 = Matthew 13:11 = Luke 8:10. "Do not let . . .": compare Matthew 6:3.

63: Parable of the Rich Fool: compare Luke 12:16–21. "Whoever has ears . . .": see 8 and the note.

64: Parable of the Great Banquet: compare Luke 14:16–24 = Matthew 22:1–10.

65: Parable of the Vineyard: compare Mark 12:1–9 = Matthew 21:33–41 = Luke 20:9–16. "Perhaps the servant did not know them": possibly correct to "Perhaps they did not know [or recognize] the servant." "Whoever has ears . . .": compare 8 and the note.

66: Compare Psalm 118:22; Mark 12:10 = Matthew 21:42 = Luke 20:17; Acts 4:11; 1 Peter 2:7.

67: Compare 61 and the note; also 1 Corinthians 13:2; Mark 8:36 = Matthew 16:26 = Luke 9:25.

68: Compare Matthew 5:10–11 = Luke 6:22; also saying 58. On the place of persecution as an inner place, see saying 69. An alternate understanding of the last part of 68 may yield the following meaning: "You will discover a place where you will not be persecuted," perhaps Pella in Transjordan, where Christians fleeing from Jerusalem settled at the time of the first-century c.e. revolt against the Romans.

69: On the first beatitude, see Matthew 5:10. "In their hearts": compare John 4:23–24. On the second, see Luke 6:21 = Matthew 5:6.

70: Salvation and life are achieved only when the inner, spiritual person comes to full expression. Compare also 41; 61; 67.

71: Partially restored. Compare sayings about the destruction of the Jewish temple (Mark 14:58 = Matthew 26:61; Mark 15:29 = Matthew 27:40; Acts 6:14) or the bodily temple (John 2:19).

72: Compare Luke 12:13–14.

73: A brief dialogue contrasting the small number of believers with the large number of those needing salvation; compare saying 23. "The harvest is large . . .": compare Matthew 9:37–38 = Luke 10:2. "Someone said": literally, "He said." On the saying of this person see Origen, *Against Celsus* 8.15. "Many are around the well": perhaps "many are around the drinking trough." "No one is in the well": or, "nothing is in the well." "Many are standing . . .": compare the Parable of the Wise and Foolish Young Women, Matthew 25:1–13. On "those who are alone" (the text uses the word *monachos*), see 16 and the note.

74: Parable of the Pearl: compare Matthew 13:45–46. On the saying about the treasure, see Matthew 6:19–20 = Luke 12:33; Matthew 13:44.

75: "I am the light . . .": compare John 8:12. "I am all . . .": compare Isaiah 44:6; Revelation 1:8; 22:13; also sayings 18; 49; 50; *Secret Book of John* 5:12 and the note. "Split a piece of wood . . .": the seeker may find Jesus anywhere. Jesus is omnipresent and penetrates the very fabric of this world. On splitting wood and gathering rocks, see also Ecclesiastes 10:9.

76: Compare Matthew 11:7–8 = Luke 7:24–25.

77: Compare Luke 11:27–28; 23:29; also Mark 13:17 = Matthew 24:19 = Luke 21:23.

78: Compare 56. In 56 the word for "carcass" is *ptoma*; in 78 the word for "the body" is *p-soma*.

79: Spiritual wealth in the spiritual kingdom is far superior to worldly power. Compare 2; 3; 29; 83.

80: Compare 10; 16.

81–83: Three sayings about the creation of Adam, and so humanity, in the image and likeness of God. Compare Genesis 1:26–27; *Secret Book of John* 9:1–3; saying 50.

84: Compare Matthew 8:20 = Luke 9:58. The New Testament versions of this saying do not include the final statement about "rest" (compare the note to saying 2; also 50).

85: Compare 29; 56; 78; 111. The person who bases his or her welfare—body and soul—upon the bodily world will be disappointed.

86: Compare 21; also possibly *Secret Book of John* 14:5; Mark 8:38 = Matthew 16:27 = Luke 9:26.

87: Compare Matthew 23:25–26 = Luke 11:39–41.

88: Compare Matthew 11:28–30.

89: Compare Luke 12:54–56 = Matthew 16:1–3.

90: Compare Matthew 7:7–8 = Luke 11:9–10; also sayings 2; 92.

91: Compare Matthew 7:6. The word "worthless" is a textual restoration of a small lacuna.

92: See Matthew 7:8 = Luke 11:10; saying 90.

93: Compare Matthew 5:42 = Luke 6:30; 6:34–35.

94: Parable of the Yeast: compare Matthew 13:33 = Luke 13:20–21. "Whoever has ears . . .": see 8 and the note.

95: Parable of the Jar of Flour. This parable, otherwise unknown in early Christian literature, proclaims the secrecy of the kingdom and its elusive quality. The kingdom is a hidden, fragile part of human life. It comes and goes in secret and can easily be lost.

96: Parable of the Assassin. This parable, also unknown in the New Testament and other early Christian literature, emphasizes that commitment to the kingdom requires forethought, preparation, and strength.

97: Compare Mark 3:32–35 = Matthew 12:47–50 = Luke 8:20–21.

98: Compare Mark 12:13–17 = Matthew 22:15–22 = Luke 20:20–26. The third and last of the commands ("give me what is mine") is not found in the New Testament versions of the saying, and elevates the place and significance of Jesus.

99: Compare 55 and the references in the note. Here the first two statements of the saying present a conundrum: one is to hate one's parents, and yet one is also to love one's parents. The concluding sentence resolves the riddle by positing two orders of family, and two mothers of Jesus. The lacuna may possibly be restored as follows: "For my mother brought me forth." Mary brought Jesus forth, but Jesus' "true mother" (probably the holy Spirit) provided true life. See the *Secret Book of James* 3:17 and the note concerning the Spirit as mother.

100: Compare 39. Various of Jesus' woes pronounced against the Pharisees are known in the New Testament gospels, for instance, Matthew 23:1–36 and Luke 11:37–54. The dog in the food trough is a frequent theme in folk literature.

101: Compare 21; Matthew 24:43 = Luke 12:39. "Where the robbers will enter": or, "when the robbers will enter." "Prepare for action": literally, "gird the loins." The saying is partially restored, including the word "estate."

102: Compare Mark 2:18–20 = Matthew 9:14–15 = Luke 5:33–35; also other critiques of Jewish or Jewish-Christian observance in sayings 6; 14; 27; 53.

103: This saying may be interpreted in different ways. It may refer to polemical statements about Jesus being born of a whore (see John 8:41, as well as other Jewish traditions describing Jesus as Yeshu ben Pantera, sometimes understood to be Jesus the son of Mary and a Roman soldier named Panther). A more probable interpretation is that one should despise one's physical parents; see saying 99.

104: Compare 22 and 48, and the notes on them.

105: Parable of the Lost Sheep: compare Matthew 18:12–14 = Luke 15:3–7. On the sheep being "the biggest," see the Parable of the Wise Fisher, saying 8.

106: Compare 13; John 7:37. Jesus promises to become mystically identified with the believer.

107: Parable of the Hidden Treasure: compare and contrast Matthew 13:44.

108: Compare 79.

109: Compare Isaiah 34:4; Hebrews 1:12; Revelation 6:14.

110: This saying is presented here as a separate saying, though problems remain (for instance, an idiosyncratic quotation formula, "Jesus says"). Compare 56; 78.

111: Compare 29; 85.

112: Compare 3; Luke 17:20–21.

113: In much of Gnostic literature Peter is made the advocate of harshly chauvinistic attitudes. Here Jesus' response to Peter, though shocking to modern sensitivities, is intended to be a statement of liberation. The female principle is saved when all that is earthly (that is, allied with an earth Mother) is transformed into what is heavenly (that is, allied with a heavenly Father). Thus all people on the earth, whether women or men, require such a transformation. Also see saying 7 and the note on it.

The Book of Thomas

Nag Hammadi Codex II, tractate 7
page 138, line 1, to page 145, line 19

Title. Of the two titles of the text, the first is given as a title in the manuscript and is followed by this descriptive phrase: "The contender [or champion] writing to the perfect"—hence scholars have sometimes referred to the text as the *Book of Thomas the Contender.* The second title is based on the incipit and may be an older form of the title.

1:1: Incipit, or Opening. Compare *Gospel of Thomas* Prologue. In the early church it was frequently asserted that someone named Matthew functioned as the compiler of sayings (and at times specifically secret sayings) of Jesus. See Papias (in Eusebius' *History of the Church* 3.39.16), as well as statements in Clement of Alexandria's *Miscellanies* [*Stromateis*] and Hippolytus' *Refutation of All Heresies.*

1:2–7: Speech introducing the revelatory dialogue. 3: On Judas Thomas as the brother and twin of Jesus, see *Gospel of Thomas* Prologue and the note. "My true friend": compare the role of the "beloved disciple" in the Gospel of John, and probably also in the *Secret Gospel of Mark.* A list of questions that describe what one must know in order to be saved is common in Gnostic texts. Perhaps the most famous of such lists is in Clement of Alexandria, *Excerpts of Theodotus* 78.2; compare also *Secret Book of John* 1:6–8; 17. *4–6:* Thomas is instructed to continue the quest for self-knowledge. Compare *Gospel of Thomas* 3; *Secret Book of James* 8:1 and the note. "Whoever does not know self . . .": the Coptic text has verbs in the perfect tense, literally "has (not) known."

2:1–14: *Dialogue about visible and invisible things.* 1: "Your ascension": compare *Secret Book of James* 9:8, 12; 10:1, 7; *Secret Book of John* 10:13; 16:17; Luke 24:51; Acts 1:9–11. 2: On doing or accomplishing the truth, see John 3:21; 1 John 1:6. 3–4: The contrast between the visible and the invisible is a contrast between the lower world of body, change, perishability, and animal nature, on the one hand, and the higher world of soul, constancy, immortality, and spiritual nature, on the other hand. The text admits that it is difficult to live a life based on the invisible, spiritual world. This contrast is most familiar from the discussion of the soul in Plato's *Phaedo.* On the rhetorical questions of these verses, and particularly verse 3, compare John 3:12. 5: The theme of being workers for spiritual truth ties this section of dialogue together; compare verses 2, 4, 5, 14. 7–8: Partially restored; the conclusion of verse 7 cannot be reconstructed with confidence. 10–11: Visible bodies need to eat other visible things in order to survive, and this only perpetuates the cycle of change and dissolution. 14: On still being babies, students, or apprentices (see verse 5), compare 1 Corinthians 3:1–3; Ephesians 4:13–14; Hebrews 5:12–14.

3:1–14: *Dialogue about escape from the visible world.* 1–3: Parable of the Archers. On the wording in verse 3, see 1 Corinthians 3:13. 4: It is the Savior who reveals whether or not one's life is on a proper course. Compare John 1:9; 8:12; 12:46. 6: A question about the sun. 7–8: Here and elsewhere in ancient religious literature, the spiritual and enlightened part of a person is described as being drawn to heaven by the beams of the sun. 11–12: Verse 11 is partially restored, verse 12 largely restored. 13: On the personification of wisdom, see the *Secret Book of John* 5:6 and the note. Plato and other Greek philosophers describe the soul as having wings. Similarly, the ancient Egyptians portray the soul as a bird.

4:1–19: *Dialogue about those who do not escape from the visible world.* 2: For a similar abrupt intrusion of the first-person plural "we," see John 3:11. 3: Wisdom reflections reminiscent of Proverbs and other wisdom literature. 4: Psalm 1:3. 5: Compare 3:13–14. 7–11: The imprisonment of these people is depicted in a manner that recalls Plato and the *Phaedo* once again. See especially *Phaedo* 81C–82A; 83DE. 12: The text is too badly damaged to allow for confident restoration. 13: Partly restored at the beginning; the Coptic text uses verbs in the past tense. On the stages in the quest for truth, compare

9:6–7; *Gospel of Thomas* 2. *14*: "Our own people," that is, the wise, perfect people. *16*: "Body," literally "vessel." *17*: "The faith they once had": these people have wings but do not use them, 4:5. Once they were counted as believers (compare Mark 4:18–19 = Matthew 13:22 = Luke 8:14; Revelation 2:4), but they succumbed to the fire smoldering within them. As a result, eventually they may be reincarnated; compare 9:5; *Secret Book of John* 14:17. *19*: See the *Phaedo* 81C–E.

5:1–16: Dialogue about the fate of ordinary people. 2: These people have good intentions but succumb to passion and sins of the flesh. *5*: "Kingdom," restored. These people may be ordinary believers who refuse the life of strict abstinence from the world. Their lot will not be a happy one. *8–9*: Partly restored. *14–16*: Allegory of Plant Life, also descriptive of human reproduction and life. Compare Plato's *Phaedo* 83DE; the *Homeric Hymn to Demeter*, on the life cycle of the Grain Mother and her daughter Kore as celebrated in the Eleusinian Mysteries; 1 Corinthians 15:36–38, 42–44; John 12:24. In the *Book of Thomas*, however, the allegory communicates an ascetic message: sowing and reproducing do not bring life, but rather death.

6:1–11: Dialogue about the fate of scoffers. 4–11: Portrait of Tartaros, with features typical of other depictions of the underworld. Compare Hesiod's *Theogony* 736–44; Plato's *Phaedo* 111C–114C and *Republic* 614B–621D (myth of Er); *Secret Book of John* 14:15–17, 22; Ethiopic *Apocalypse of Peter*; and Dante's *Inferno*. Verses 6–8 are partially restored; the translation of verses 7–8 remains tentative. "The rulers . . .": or, "Those who persecute you will be given over to the angel Tartarouchos."

7:1–27: Revelation of woes. In chapters 7–9, the Savior utters a series of twelve woes against those who indulge the fire and the flesh. *2*: "The prison that will perish": the body is the perishable prison of the soul in Platonic and Orphic thought. See also *Secret Book of John* 11:5; 13:14. *9*: The image of prisoners in caves recalls the description of people bound in the cave in Plato's *Republic* 514AB. *13*: "The poisoning . . .": or "your crowning achievement, the beating by your enemies" (literally, "the beating of your enemies"). *16–17*: Partially restored; the conclusion of 17 cannot be reconstructed with any certainty. "The filthy clothing you are wearing" is the body, which is put on and taken off like an article of clothing. Compare *Secret Book of James* 7:13 and the note; *Gospel of Thomas* 21; 37; *Secret Book of John* 11:1–6. *20–21*: Compare the role of the sun (and moon) in 7:27 and 8:1–6. *22*: Compare *Gospel of Thomas* 113 and the note.

8:1–6: *Revelation about salvation and light.* 1: The "sweet smell" of salvation is granted to people, and to the elements. On the elements see *Secret Book of John* 11:3–4; 13:10. Here spirit is substituted for fire as one of the four elements, since fire is characteristic of passion, lust, and destruction throughout the present text. 2–6: Parable of the Grapevine and the Weeds. What lives in the light grows vigorously, and rules triumphantly over the darkness. Compare also *Gospel of Thomas* 40 and the note.

9:1–7: *Conclusion of the revelation.* 1: The twelfth and final woe: compare 7:1–27. Several lines are too badly damaged to be restored. 3: Compare Matthew 5:11 = Luke 6:22; *Gospel of Thomas* 68; 69. 4: Compare Luke 6:21 = Matthew 5:4. "Without hope," that is, without the hope of salvation. 5: "Watch and pray," compare Mark 14:38 = Matthew 26:41. One must escape the grim realities of incarnation and reincarnation; compare 4:17. 6–7: On the stages in the process of salvation (pray, find rest, reign), see 4:13; *Gospel of Thomas* 2.

The Secret Book of John

Nag Hammadi Codex II, tractate 1
page 1, line 1, to page 32, line 9

1:1: *Incipit, or Opening.* While the title of the text (*Secret Book [Apokryphon] of John*) is given in the manuscripts, the poorly preserved incipit may also refer to the text as "the teaching of the Savior" and possibly "the revelation" (if the restoration adopted here is accurate).

1:2–18: *Introduction to the revelatory appearance of the Savior.* 2: John the son of Zebedee is confronted by a Pharisee. The name Arimanios is probably taken from the evil spirit of Zoroastrian fame, Ahriman. 3: Compare *Secret Book of James* 4:13; 5:3; 9:8; John 17:5. 5: One version of the text (Berlin Gnostic Codex 8502) specifically states that John went onto a mountain. In numerous ancient and modern traditions, visions and religious experiences are described as taking place on mountains, where one is in solitude, removed from mundane affairs, and close to the divine. 6–8: A list of questions summarizing what one must know for salvation. Other Gnostic texts also include such lists of questions; compare the indirect questions in the *Book of Thomas* 1:3, as well as in the present text, 1:17. Here the list functions as a table of contents for the text. 7–8: "Eternal realm," *aeon* here and elsewhere in the translation. 9: The glorious vision of the luminous being is accompanied by apocalyptic phenomena: the heavens open (compare Mark 1:10 = Matthew 3:16 = Luke 3:21; John 1:51; Acts 7:55–56; Revelation 4:1; 19:11) and the world is illuminated and shaken (compare *Secret Book of James* 10:2; Mark 13:8, 24–26 = Matthew 24:7, 29–30 = Luke 21:11, 25–27). 10–13: The luminous figure of the Savior changes from one form to another. 15–16: Revelatory "I am" statements (compare the Gospel of John and numerous Gnostic texts; also Matthew 28:19–20), and the disclosure of the divine triad of Father, Mother, Child. 17: See 1:6–8 and the note; *Book of Thomas* 1:3. 18: "The unshakable race," the phrase used to describe the Gnostic group. These people cannot be shaken, and do not waver, in their quest for truth. See also 14:2; 15:14; 16:18.

2:1–22: *Revelation about the One.* A classic statement of divine transcendence, formulated with terms of negation. Compare the *via negativa* of the *Upanishads*, with the insistence that the Ultimate is *neti neti*, "not this, not that." 2: The One may be considered as Father, the first in the divine triad. 3: "The invisible Spirit," a common designation for the One (compare 3:5, 7, 9, 12, 13, 14, 15, 16, etc.). It is beyond deity. 10: It is beyond perfection, or any other finite category. 13: It is beyond being, as the ground of all being. 14: It is the wholly other. 18: Compare *Secret Book of James* 1:1. 20: Finally, it can only be said that the One is in silence, at rest, before all. The divine Silence is a common image in mystical traditions. 22: Several lines of the text are rather badly damaged, and a portion cannot be reconstructed with confidence. This verse suggests that the ineffable Father can be known in a limited way only because a revealer has come forth from the Father. Compare John 1:18.

3:1–18: *Revelation about the divine Mother.* 1–2: Partly restored. The Perfect One (text: "it" or "he") gazes into the water and falls in love with its own image, much as Narcissus does in Greek mythology (compare Ovid, *Metamorphoses* 3.402–510). Contrast the bastardization of the process in the creative activities of Yaldabaoth, 8:14–15 along with 9:1. 3: As the result of this love, the Father's Mind produces a Thought (*Ennoia*), who is the divine Mother. For other examples of such acts of independent procreation on the part of father-gods, compare especially the Greek god Zeus, who produces Athena, the daughter of Metis ("Wisdom," or "Skill"), from his head alongside the River (or Lake) Triton (see Hesiod, *Theogony* 886–900, 924–29); also the Egyptian god Atum, who creates by means of masturbation. *4:* She is Forethought, *Pronoia.* *6:* Barbelo, a name probably of Hebrew derivation but of uncertain meaning, perhaps something like "God in Four" (that is, the tetragrammaton). *8:* "The common Parent," *Metropator,* sometimes translated as "grandfather" but possibly understood here as "Mother-Father," or androgynous Parent. "Triple" and "male" are symbolic terms employed to emphasize the complete and heavenly character of Barbelo. Compare *Gospel of Thomas* 113 and the note, on "male" as a term describing what is heavenly. *9–16:* With the agreement of the invisible Spirit, four spiritual beings come from Thought (Barbelo): Foreknowledge, Imperishability, Life Eternal, and Truth. *17:* Together with Barbelo these four constitute the realm (*aeon*) of the Five. *18:* The Five, being androgynous, can also be termed the Ten. This realm is the Father in emanation.

4:1–16: Revelation about the divine Child. *1–3:* Pure, spiritual intercourse between the Father and Barbelo produces a Child of light. *5–6:* The Child is anointed by the Father (compare the Messiah, or Christ, as the anointed one). *7–8:* Mind, *Nous,* joins the Child as a co-worker. "Christ," or "the Good One": compare the anointing with goodness in 4:5. *9:* Creation by the word (compare Genesis 1; John 1:1–3; Hebrews 11:3) may now take place. *11:* "The self-produced God": the divine *Autogenes,* or self-begotten one. For the general wording, compare John 1:3. *15:* Genesis 1:26; Psalm 8, especially 8:5–8; 1 Corinthians 15:24–28. *16:* "A name greater than every name": compare Philippians 2:9; Ephesians 1:21; Hebrews 1:4. This exalted universe is the realm of the divine; compare 1:8.

5:1–17: Revelation about the four stars. *1:* The Child produces the stars by means of a creative gaze. *3–6:* The four stars (Armozel, Oroiel, Daveithai, Eleleth) each are represented by three personages; "Afterthought" (verse 4) is a translation of *Epinoia.* The twelfth and last of these personages is Sophia, "Wisdom." On Wisdom in the Bible see Proverbs 8; Matthew 11:19 = Luke 7:35; Luke 11:49 (contrast Matthew 23:34); 1 Corinthians 1:18–2:13; Romans 11:33; Colossians 2:3; Ephesians 3:10; and various passages in the Wisdom of Solomon and Sirach. In several of the Christian passages there is a close relationship between Wisdom and Christ. *9–11:* The creation of Pigeradamas, "Adam the Stranger," where "stranger" (Hebrew *ger*) designates one who is an alien and sojourner in this world but at home in heaven. See *Secret Book of James* 7:4–6. *12*: Compare *Gospel of Thomas* 18; 49; 50; 1 Corinthians 8:6; Romans 11:36; Colossians 1:16; Hebrews 2:10. *13*: "The three": compare 1:16. *14*: Seth: see 13:15–16; Genesis 4:25–26; 5:1–8. *15*: "The family [or seed] of Seth": the spiritual descendents of the luminous race above. Compare "the unshakable race" (1:18 and the note).

6:1–9: Revelation about the fall of Sophia. Compare the Greek goddess Hera, who imitates Zeus and brings forth a child by herself. According to one version of the myth, the child is the terrible monster Typhon (*Homeric Hymn to Pythian Apollo* 300–62). According to another, it is the lame god Hephaestus, whom Hera evicts from Olympus and sends down to this world below (Hesiod, *Theogony* 924–29). The artisan among the gods, Hephaestus is represented in Egyptian mythology by his counterpart Ptah, the creator-god and divine craftsman of Memphis. *1*: The procreative act is Sophia's own responsibility, yet the invisible Spirit also reflects upon it. Thus the author struggles with the issue of theodicy. Evil does finally derive from the divine realm above, but the scandal of this admission is mitigated by the suggestion that Sophia, as the last emanation of the divine (5:6), made an innocent mistake (compare 12:9), but not without the foreknowledge of the invisible Spirit. *5*: Some texts (for example, the version of the *Secret Book of John* in Berlin Gnostic Codex 8502) refer to this as Sophia's abortion. *6*: A number of ancient texts depict the demiurge with leonine features; also see *Gospel of Thomas* 7. *8*: "Mother of the Living": Genesis 3:20 (compare, below, 12:9 plus 10:12; 13:6). *9*: Yaldabaoth: the meaning of the name is unknown; one suggestion is "Child of Chaos."

7:1–30: Revelation about the establishment of the cosmic bureaucracy. *1*: Yaldabaoth steals from his Mother (a further vindication of the innocence of Sophia; see 6:1 and the note) and moves away. *3*: "Mindlessness," *Aponoia*. *4–7*: The twelve cosmic authorities probably correspond to the signs of the Zodiac. Some of the names are familiar from the Hebrew Bible (Adonaios, Sabaoth, Cain, Abel); most of the others clearly are derived from Hebrew. *8*: "Seven kings," for the seven planetary and astral spheres posited by ancient astronomers. *9*: The spiritual light from the Mother remains with Yaldabaoth alone. *12*: Saklas, perhaps "Fool." Samael, perhaps "Blind God."

13: Isaiah 45:5–6; 46:9; compare 7:29 below. *14:* The number of angels corresponds to the number of days in the solar year; compare 9:35. *16–18:* The list of seven potentates represents the days in a week and in part repeats the list of authorities in 7:4–7. "Yao" is a common form of the ineffable Hebrew name of God. "Yao Sabaoth" reflects the Hebrew for "the Lord of Hosts." *27–28:* The cosmic bureaucracy below is an imitation of the heavenly realms above. Yaldabaoth has the power to copy the heavenly pattern because of the Mother's spirit within him. *29:* Exodus 20:5; 34:14; Isaiah 45: 5–6; 46:9; compare 7:13 above.

8:1–15: Revelation about the repentance of Sophia and the appearance of Humanity. *2–4:* Genesis 1:2: the spirit of God moving above the waters. *6–8:* Sophia repents and is partially restored. She receives some divine Fullness as her lover comes to her at last. *9:* Her final restoration will occur when the spirit she lost to Yaldabaoth is retrieved. Until then, she is to dwell in the ninth sphere just above Yaldabaoth, who occupies the eighth sphere and thus rules over the seven kings below him (7:8). *13:* In Coptic the pronouns used here are masculine, probably because "Parent" and "first Humanity" are masculine terms. *14–15:* In a parody of the original creative act of the Perfect One (3:1–2), Yaldabaoth and his authorities look at the waters above the earth (compare Genesis 1:7), and from the bottom they see the image of Humanity.

9:1–36: Revelation about the creation of the psychical human body. The lists of angels in the translation have been compiled by means of a comparison of the versions in Codex II and Codex IV. *1:* Genesis 1:26.7–17: The psychical body is a balanced, androgynous body, with both female and male sexual organs (compare verse 15). The names of some of the angels are recognizably Hebraic. These verses could also be translated as follows: "The first angel began by creating the head: Eteraphaope-Abron; another created the top of the head: Meniggesstroeth; another created the brain: Asterechme; the right eye: Thaspomocha"; and so forth, through verse 17. This translation would solve the problem posed by the awkward conclusion to verse 17 (thus: "its toes: Miamai; the toenails: Labernioum"). *18:* Compare 7:4–6. *19–34:* Additional lists of angels, demons, and demonic passions. Some of the names seem Semitic; a few are familiar (verse 24, for example). *35:* See 7:14. As in certain magical texts, the number of angels and the number of parts in the human body is three hundred sixty-five. 36: "The Book of Zoroaster": compare the text *Zostrianos* from Codex VIII of the Nag Hammadi library, as well as Porphyry's *Life of Plotinus* 16, where the author refers to other texts written under the name of the Persian sage Zoroaster, including a Book of Zoroaster.

10:1–14: *Revelation about the salvific subterfuge.* 1: Without the spirit of Sophia the psychical human body has no vitality. 3: "Five stars": probably the four stars of 5:1–8, together with the Child (Christ) who produced them. 6: Genesis 2:7. 8: On movement as the result of the divine spirit within, see 14:9; *Gospel of Thomas* 50. 9–10: Adam, enlightened with spiritual power, is thrown down into the depths of the cosmos. 12: Afterthought, or *Epinoia*, appears again, now in order to restore the dimmed light below to the fullness of light above. Compare Genesis 2:18–22; 3:20. "Life" is *Zoe*, Eve. 13: The "way of ascent," the restoration of the light, follows the "way of descent," the fall of the light.

11:1–23: *Revelation about the imprisonment of humanity.* 3: The four elements, with "fiery winds" replacing air; compare 11:4 and 13:10 (wind instead of air); also *Book of Thomas* 8:1 (spirit instead of fire). The noise is that of the workshop where a statue or a fetter is being forged. 4: The rulers manufacture another body for Adam, a mortal body of flesh. 5: The body as the prison or tomb of the soul is a well-known Platonic and Orphic doctrine. 6: Adam's plight is the paradigm of human estrangement from the divine realm. 8: Genesis 2:8–9, 16. 10: Genesis 2:9. 12–13: The rulers' Tree of Life is as deadly as they are. 14: Genesis 2:9, 17; 3:3. As also at 12:11, Afterthought assumes the form of a tree, just as Daphne in Greek mythology changes into a laurel tree (Ovid, *Metamorphoses* 1.452–567). See the *Reality of the Rulers* (Nag Hammadi Codex II, tractate 4), page 89, lines 17–28; and *On the Origin of the World* (tractate 5), page 116, lines 25–33. 15: Genesis 3:5–7. 17: Genesis 3:1–5. 22: Genesis 2:21. 23: Isaiah 6:10 (quoted in Matthew 13:14–15; John 12:40; Acts 28:26–27; compare Mark 4:12 = Matthew 13:13 = Luke 8:10). "The first ruler": the text has only "he" or "it"; possibly read "Thus it is said in the prophet."

12:1–14: *Revelation about the separation of Adam and Eve.* 1–4: Genesis 2:21–22. 6–8: Genesis 2:23–24. 9: See 6:8; 10:12; Genesis 3:20. Here Sophia takes the role assigned to Afterthought in 10:12–14. On their close identification, see 6:1. Sophia is both the one who is saved and the one who saves. *10*: "The Living," the Gnostics. *11*: See 11:14 and the note. The Savior ("I") appears as a heavenly bird (the eagle is the royal bird of Zeus) to bring the human beings to knowledge. Compare the heavenly letter in the Hymn of the Pearl within the *Acts of Thomas*: the letter sent from the king of the East (that is, God) flies as an eagle, and upon landing it becomes an enlightening voice of revelation. *13*: Genesis 3:7.

13:1–18: Revelation about the abuse of Adam and Eve. 1: Genesis 3:14–19. *2*: Compare 10:2–4. The mystery of which Yaldabaoth is unaware is the heavenly decision to manipulate cosmic affairs for the purpose of the recovery of the spiritual light. *4*: Genesis 3:23–24. *7*: The rape of Eve is also discussed in the *Reality of the Rulers*, page 89, lines 17–31; and *On the Origin of the World*, page 116, line 8, to page 117, line 28. Elohim (Coptic: *Eloim*) is Hebrew for "God"; Yahweh (Coptic: *Yawe*) is the ineffable name of God in Hebrew. *11*: Cain and Abel (also the names of two of the authorities of Yaldabaoth, 7:5–6; 9:18) thus are not children of Adam and Eve, but of Yaldabaoth and Eve. Compare Genesis 4:1–2. *14*: "Bodily tomb": see 11:5. *15*: Genesis 4:25; 5:3; on the heavenly child named Seth, see above, 5:14. *17*: "Water of forgetfulness": compare the water of the River Lethe in the Greek conception of the underworld. If the thirsty soul drinks of the water of Lethe, it forgets about its previous lives and may be reincarnated in yet another body. *18*: The divine purpose behind the vicissitudes of human life is declared once again.

14:1–22: Questions and revelatory answers about the destinies of human beings. Throughout this section the soul (*psyche*) is depicted, in the usual fashion of Greek and Gnostic literature, as a woman. Compare the myth of Psyche and Eros (or Cupid, Love) in Apuleius' *Metamorphoses* books 4–6, and the Gnostic version of the myth in the Nag Hammadi text *Exegesis on the Soul* (Codex II, tractate 6). *2*: "The unshakable race": see 1:18. *3–6*: The spiritual people who live from above. "Those who receive them" (verse 5) are probably the Imperishable Ones of the heavenly realms (see 13:18; *Book of Thomas* 3:8), or else the cosmic rulers who take back the flesh (see *Gospel of Thomas* 21; 86). For parallels to the motifs in verse 6, compare Wisdom of Solomon 4:2; 1 Corinthians 9:24–27; 13:7; 1 Timothy 6:12; 2 Timothy 4:7–8; Hebrews 12:1. *7–13*: Souls with spiritual possibilities who turn to the life of the spirit. On power descending upon everyone (verse 9), see 10:1–8. *14–20*: Souls with spiritual possibilities who indulge the contemptible spirit. After going through reincarnation (verse 17; compare *Book of Thomas* 4:17; 9:5), such a soul may finally be saved by following those who live the life of the spirit (verse 20). On the soul becoming youthful again and returning to the Mother's womb (literally "nature," verse 18), compare John 3:4; *Gospel of Thomas* 22. 21–22: Souls who reject knowledge. Such people, who have committed blasphemy against the Spirit (compare Mark 3:28–29 = Matthew 12:31–32 = Luke 12:10; *Gospel of Thomas* 44), will be punished eternally.

15:1–25: *Revelation about the final plots against humanity.* 6–10: The sexual violation of Sophia and subsequent production of Fate (*Heimarmene*), the inexorable power of terrestrial and astrological bondage. 11–15: The first ruler sends a great flood upon the world. Compare Genesis 6:5–8:22; 7:7 is cited in verse 13. "Those who were strangers" to enlightened Noah (verse 12) are those who identify with this world but are estranged from the heavenly realm (contrast 5:9–11 and the note). On "the unshakable race" (verse 14), see also 1:18 and the note. 16–25: The angels of the first ruler take human women, and lead them into childbirth and enslavement. Compare Genesis 6:1–4; 1 *Enoch* 6–11. This process, the text concludes, continues to the present day (verses 23 and 25).

16:1–16: *Hymn of the Savior.* The Savior claims to be Forethought, and identifies with several descents of Forethought into this world. Who is this Savior who reveals self? In the broader context of the *Secret Book of John* the Savior is Christ. As Christ, the Savior who descends into the world may be compared with Christ descending into hell in other early Christian thought (for example, 1 Peter 3: 18–20, or the Apostles' Creed). The Hymn of the Savior may also be analyzed independently, however, since this hymn is a separable section of the text, found only in the longer versions in Codex II and Codex IV. Taken by itself, the hymn may be understood to proclaim that the Savior is the heavenly Mother: Forethought, Afterthought, Sophia. On the relationship between Wisdom and Christ in Christian texts, see above, the note to 5:3–6. Mention may also be made of similar connections between Wisdom and Christ in other Christian Gnostic documents. 1: The Savior is essentially identical with the subsequent offspring of light. 3–4: The first descent, exemplified in the earlier accounts of Sophia and Adam, constitutes the fall and incarceration of the light hidden in the world and the body below. The ignorant powers of this world do not recognize the spiritual light; compare 10:6. *5–8*: The second descent is undertaken in order to begin a task: the restoration and salvation of the light. Compare the prominent saving roles of Afterthought and Sophia in the earlier accounts, and the sending of Life to help the light below (10:11–14; 12:1, 5, 9–10). Life is snatched out of this world, however, at an appropriate time, 13:6. *9–16*: The third descent involves the sending of the heavenly call to rouse the prototypal sleeper from ignorance to the knowledge of salvation. On the description of the Savior who is issuing the call (verse 10), see John 1:14.

16:17–19: Conclusion to the revelatory appearance of the Savior. *17*: The revelation concludes with the Savior announcing the return to the heavenly realm (compare *Secret Book of James* 9:8, 12; 10:1, 7; *Book of Thomas* 2:1). *18–19*: On the care required for the communication of these teachings, see *Secret Book of James* 1:3; Revelation 22:18–19. On "the unshakable race" see 1:18 and the note.

16:20–21: Close of the text. Compare *Secret Book of James* 10:1, 6–7. John repeats the mystery of the Savior to the disciples. The manuscripts (Codex II and Codex IV) add a few final words of Christian devotion.

BIBLIOGRAPHY

Introduction

Although the number of books and articles published on Gnosticism and the Nag Hammadi library is large, a professional bibliographer, David M. Scholer, has facilitated the task of locating the relevant literature in Nag Hammadi studies by publishing a book that provides a classified listing of such works: *Nag Hammadi Bibliography 1948–1969* (Nag Hammadi Studies 1; Leiden: Brill, 1971). Updated annually in the autumn issue of the periodical *Novum Testamentum*, Scholer's bibliography soon will appear in a second volume.

Several fine introductions to Gnosticism and the Nag Hammadi texts are available, including Hans Jonas, *The Gnostic Religion* (Boston: Beacon, 1963); Elaine H. Pagels, *The Gnostic Gospels* (New York: Random House, 1979); James M. Robinson's "Introduction" to *The Nag Hammadi Library in English*, ed. by Robinson and Marvin W. Meyer (San Francisco: Harper & Row; Leiden: Brill, 1977), pp. 1–25; and Kurt Rudolph, *Die Gnosis* (Leipzig: Koehler & Amelang, 1977), published in English translation as *Gnosis* (San Francisco: Harper & Row, 1983). Other extremely helpful analyses may be found in James M. Robinson and Helmut Koester, *Trajectories through Early Christianity* (Philadelphia: Fortress, 1971). For a survey of the archeological work undertaken near the site of the discovery of the Nag Hammadi library, see especially the articles in the fall 1979 issue of *Biblical Archeologist*.

The translations given here are based upon the Coptic texts as presented in two sets of volumes being produced by the Coptic Gnostic Library Project of the Institute for Antiquity and Christianity, Claremont Graduate School: *The Facsimile Edition of the Nag Hammadi Codices*, published under the auspices of the Department of Antiquities of the Arab Republic of Egypt in conjunction with UNESCO (Leiden: Brill, 1972–), with magnificent photographs of the pages, covers, and cartonnage of the Nag Hammadi codices; and *The Coptic Gnostic Library*, a subseries of Nag Hammadi Studies (Leiden: Brill, 1975–), with Coptic texts, English translations, notes, and indices. The three volumes of *The Coptic Gnostic Library* that pertain to our four texts are all forthcoming: *Nag Hammadi Codex I (The Jung Codex)*, ed. by Harold W. Attridge; *Nag Hammadi Codex II, 2–7*, ed. by Bentley Layton; and *Nag Hammadi Codices II,1, III,1, and IV,1 with Papyrus Berolinensis 8502,2: The Apocryphon of John*, ed. by Frederik Wisse.

On the use of inclusive language, see Joann Haugerud, *The Word for Us* (Seattle: Coalition on Women and Religion, 1977); Letty M. Russell, *The Liberating Word* (Philadelphia: Westminster, 1976); *She Said/He Said: An Annotated Bibliography of Sex Differences in Language, Speech, and Nonverbal Communication*, compiled by Nancy Henley and Barrie Thorne (Pittsburgh: Know, 1975); and *An Inclusive Language Lectionary: Readings for Year A* (National Council of Churches; Atlanta: John Knox; Philadelphia: Westminster; New York: Pilgrim, 1983).

For discussions of sayings of Jesus in the *Secret Book of James*, the *Gospel of Thomas*, and the *Book of Thomas*, see particularly Helmut Koester, "Apocryphal and Canonical Gospels," *Harvard Theological Review* 73 (1980) 105–30; "Dialog und Spruchüberlieferung in den gnostischen Texten von Nag Hammadi," *Evangelische Theologie* 39 (1979) 532–56; "Gnostic Writings as Witnesses for the Development of the Sayings Tradition," in *The Rediscovery of Gnosticism*, ed. by Bentley Layton (Leiden: Brill, 1980), vol. 1, pp. 238–61; Hans-Martin Schenke, "The Book of Thomas (NHC II.7): A Revision of a Pseudepigraphical Letter of Jacob the Contender," a paper presented during the autumn of 1982 and recently published in *The New Testament and Gnosis*, ed. by A. J. M. Wedderburn and A. H. B. Logan (Edinburgh: T. & T. Clark, 1983); and Charles W. Hedrick, "Kingdom Sayings and Parables of Jesus in *The Apocryphon of James*: Tradition and Redaction," *New Testament Studies* 29 (1983) 1–24. Koester also considers the Nag Hammadi text entitled *Dialogue of the Savior* (Codex III, tractate 5) to be significant for the development of traditions having to do with sayings of Jesus. This text is not included in the present volume of translations because of its fragmentary character; it may be read in *The Nag Hammadi Library in English*, pp. 229–38, and is reprinted in *The Other Gospels*, ed. by Ron Cameron (Philadelphia: Westminster, 1982), pp. 38–48. On methods and criteria to be employed for identifying teachings of the historical Jesus, see Norman Perrin and Dennis C. Duling, *The New Testament: An Introduction* (New York: Harcourt Brace Jovanovich, 1982), pp. 397–429.

On the character of Jewish Christianity and its relationship to Gnosticism, see Alexander Böhlig, "Der jüdische und judenchristliche Hintergrund in gnostischen Texten von Nag Hammadi," in *Le Origini dello Gnosticismo*, ed. by Ugo Bianchi (Leiden: Brill, 1967), pp. 109–40; Gilles Quispel, "Gnosticism and the New Testament," *Vigiliae Christianae* 19 (1965) 65–85; Hans-Joachim Schoeps, *Jewish Christianity* (Philadelphia: Fortress, 1969); and R. McL. Wilson, "Jewish Christianity and Gnosticism," *Recherches de Science Religieuse* 60 (1972) 261–72.

The Secret Book of James

The most significant study to date on the *Secret Book of James* is the elegant—and expensive—French edition by Michel Malinine, Henri-Charles Puech, Gilles Quispel, Walter C. Till, and Rodolphe Kasser, with R. McL. Wilson and Jan Zandee, *Epistula Iacobi Apocrypha* (Zürich and Stuttgart: Rascher, 1968). Other English translations of the text are those of Francis E. Williams in *The Nag Hammadi Library in English*, pp. 29–36; and Ron Cameron in *The Other Gospels*, pp. 55–64. Among the various contributions concerning this document, the following are important: James Brashler and Marvin W. Meyer, "James in the Nag Hammadi Library" (unpublished paper presented at the 1979 annual meeting of the Society of Biblical Literature, New York); S. Kent Brown, "James: A Religio-Historical Study of the Relations between Jewish, Gnostic, and Catholic Christianity in the Early Period through an Investigation of the Traditions about James the Lord's Brother" (Ph.D. dissertation, Brown University, 1972); Ron Cameron, "Sayings Traditions in the Apocryphon of James" (Ph.D. dissertation, Harvard University, 1983; forthcoming in the series Harvard Theological Studies); Kaikhohen Kipgen, "Gnosticism in Early Christianity: A Study of the Epistula Iacobi Apocrypha with Particular Reference to Salvation" (Ph.D. dissertation, Oxford University, 1975); Pheme Perkins, "Johannine Traditions in *Ap. Jas.* (NHC I,2)," *Journal of Biblical Literature* 101

(1982) 403–14; Henri-Charles Puech, "The Apocryphon of James (Apocryphon Jacobi)," in *New Testament Apocrypha,* ed. by Edgar Hennecke, Wilhelm Schneemelcher, and R. McL. Wilson (Philadelphia: Westminster, 1963), vol. 1, pp. 333–38; Hans-Martin Schenke, "Der Jakobusbrief aus dem Codex Jung," *Orientalistische Literaturzeitung* 66 (1971) 117–30; W. C. van Unnik, "The Origin of the Recently Discovered 'Apocryphon Jacobi,'" *Vigiliae Christianae* 10 (1956) 149–56; and Jan Zandee, "Gnostische trekken in een Apocryphe Brief van Jacobus," *Nederlands Theologisch Tijdschrift* 17 (1963) 401–22.

The Gospel of Thomas

No text in the Nag Hammadi library has prompted more discussion and reflection than the *Gospel of Thomas.* Currently the most accessible edition of the Coptic text with English translation is that of Antoine Guillaumont, Henri-Charles Puech, Gilles Quispel, Walter C. Till, and Yassah 'Abd al-Masih, *The Gospel according to Thomas* (New York: Harper & Row; Leiden: Brill, 1959). Two other English translations that are in print are by Thomas O. Lambdin, in *The Nag Hammadi Library in English,* pp. 117–30 (reprinted in *The Other Gospels,* pp. 23–37); and by David R. Cartlidge and David L. Dungan, in their *Documents for the Study of the Gospels* (Philadelphia: Fortress, 1980), pp. 25–35. A good study of the *Gospel of Thomas* in relation to the Oxyrhynchus Papyrus fragments is by M. Marcovich, "Textual Criticism on the *Gospel of Thomas,*" *Journal of Theological Studies* 20 n.s. (1969) 53–74.

Some of the most helpful books and commentaries on the *Gospel of Thomas* are the following: Stevan Davies, *The Gospel of Thomas and Christian Wisdom* (New York: Seabury, 1983); Bertil Gärtner, *The Theology of the Gospel according to Thomas* (New York: Harper & Row, 1961); Robert M. Grant and David Noel Freedman, *The Secret Sayings of Jesus* (Garden City, N.Y.: Doubleday, 1960); Jacques-É. Ménard, *L'Évangile selon Thomas* (Nag Hammadi Studies 5; Leiden: Brill, 1975); and Wolfgang Schrage, *Das Verhältnis des Thomas-Evangeliums zur synoptischen Tradition und zu den koptischen Evangelienübersetzungen* (Berlin: Töpelmann, 1964). For a shorter but substantial introduction to the *Gospel of Thomas,* see Henri-Charles Puech, "The Gospel of Thomas," in *New Testa-*

ment Apocrypha, vol. 1, pp. 278–307. Gilles Quispel also provides some interesting perspectives in his long review article "The *Gospel of Thomas* Revisited," in *Colloque international sur les Textes de Nag Hammadi*, ed. by Bernard Barc (Bibliothèque copte de Nag Hammadi; Quebec: L'Université Laval, 1981), pp. 218–66.

For more particular problems in the text, see such studies as Harold W. Attridge, "The Original Text of Gos. Thom., Saying 30," *Bulletin of the American Society of Papyrologists* 16 (1979) 153–57; "Greek Equivalents of Two Coptic Phrases: CG I,*1*.65,9–10 and CG II,2.43.26," *Bulletin of the American Society of Papyrologists* 18 (1981) 27–32; Howard M. Jackson, "The Lion Becomes Man: The Gnostic Leontomorphic Creator and the Platonic Tradition" (Ph.D. dissertation, Claremont Graduate School, 1983); A. F. J. Klijn, "The 'Single One' in the Gospel of Thomas," *Journal of Biblical Literature* 81 (1962) 271–78; Marvin W. Meyer, "Making Mary Male: The Categories 'Male' and 'Female' in the Gospel of Thomas," *New Testament Studies* (forthcoming); and Philipp Vielhauer, "ANAPAUSIS: Zum gnostischen Hintergrund des Thomasevangeliums," in *Apophoreta: Festschrift für Ernst Haenchen zu seinem siebzigsten Geburtstag am 10. Dezember 1964*, ed. by Walther Eltester and Franz Heinrich Kettler (Berlin: Töpelmann, 1964), pp. 281–99.

The Book of Thomas

The most complete study of the *Book of Thomas* is that of John D. Turner, *The Book of Thomas the Contender from Codex II of the Cairo Gnostic Library from Nag Hammadi* (CG II,7) (Missoula, Mont.: Scholars, 1975), an edition with text, translation, commentary, and indices. Turner has also published a revised English translation in *The Nag Hammadi Library in English*, pp. 118–94. Two studies by members of the Berlin *Arbeitskreis* are of considerable value: Dankwart Kirchner, "Das Buch des Thomas: Die siebte Schrift aus Nag-Hammadi-Codex II eingeleitet und übersetzt vom Berliner Arbeitskreis für koptisch-gnostische Schriften," *Theologische Literaturzeitung* 102 (1977) 793–804; and Hans-Martin Schenke, "The Book of Thomas (NHC II.7): A Revision of a Pseudepigraphical Letter of Jacob the Contender," part of Schenke's continuing work on this text.

The Secret Book of John

Four different texts of the *Secret Book of John* exist, three in the Nag Hammadi library (Codex II, tractate 1; Codex III, tractate 1; and Codex IV, tractate 1), and one in the Berlin Gnostic Codex 8502 (tractate 2). The present translation is based mainly on the longer version as preserved in Nag Hammadi Codex II. Reconstructions have been made by means of a comparison with the other text representing the longer version (Codex IV), as well as the two texts representing the shorter version. Such a comparison is especially vital for the opening pages of the Codex II text, which are not well preserved. The three texts of the *Secret Book of John* from the Nag Hammadi codices are published in the German edition of Martin Krause and Pahor Labib, *Die drei Versionen des Apokryphon des Johannes im koptischen Museum zu Alt-Kairo* (Abhandlungen des Deutschen Archäologischen Instituts Kairo; Wiesbaden: Harrassowitz, 1962). The text from Codex II is also available in the unreliable English edition of Søren Giversen, *Apocryphon Johannis* (Acta Theologica Danica; Copenhagen: Munksgaard, 1963). For an excellent edition of Berlin Gnostic Codex 8502, see *Die gnostischen Schriften des koptischen Papyrus Berolinensis 8502*, ed. by Walter C. Till and Hans-Martin Schenke (Texte und Untersuchungen; Berlin: Akademie, 1972). Additional English translations of the *Secret Book of John* include a translation by Martin Krause of the Berlin Gnostic Codex version, in *Gnosis*, ed. by Werner Foerster (Oxford: Clarendon, 1972), vol. 1, pp. 100–20 (published along with a closely related heresiological account written by Irenaeus of Lyons, *Against Heresies* 1.29.1–4); and a translation by Frederik Wisse primarily of the Codex II version, in *The Nag Hammadi Library in English*, pp. 98–116.

For introductions to the *Secret Book of John* one may consult Henri-Charles Puech, "The Apocryphon of John," in *New Testament Apocrypha*, vol. 1, pp. 314–31; and Frederik Wisse, "Apocryphon of John," in *The Interpreter's Dictionary of the Bible* (Nashville: Abingdon, 1976), supplementary vol., pp. 481–82. On the Sophia myth, see James E. Goehring, "A Classical Influence on the Gnostic Sophia Myth," *Vigiliae Christianae* 35 (1981) 16–23; George W. MacRae, "The Jewish Background of the Gnostic Sophia Myth," *Novum Testamentum* 12 (1970) 86–101; Marvin W. Meyer, *The*

Letter of Peter to Philip (Chico, Calif.: Scholars, 1981), pp. 121–28; and G. C. Stead, "The Valentinian Myth of Sophia," *Journal of Theological Studies* 20 n.s. (1969) 75–104. On Pigeradamas, and Afterthought becoming a tree, see Howard M. Jackson, "Geradamas, the Celestial Stranger," *New Testament Studies* 27 (1981) 385–94; and Birger A. Pearson, " 'She Became a Tree'—A Note to CG II,4: 89,25–26," *Harvard Theological Review* 69 (1976) 413–15.

About the Translator

MARVIN W. MEYER is a graduate of Calvin Theological Seminary and Claremont Graduate School. He has held positions at Barnard College, the University of California at Santa Barbara, Claremont Graduate School, and Chapman College, where he currently teaches. In addition to spending several seasons in archeological work near Nag Hammadi, Egypt and serving as an editor of *The Nag Hammadi Library in English*, he has published three books. He lives with his family in Orange, California.